AUDIO ACCESS
INCLUDED

**PLAYBACK+**
eed • Pitch • Balance • Loop

# COUNTRY CLASSICS
## FOR
# BANJO

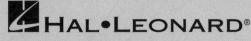

To access audio visit:
www.halleonard.com/mylibrary

Enter Code
2069-2712-8360-4773

Arranged and recorded by Michael J. Miles
Recording engineer and bass player: John Abbey

ISBN 978-1-5400-8137-7

**HAL•LEONARD®**

Visit Hal Leonard Online at
**www.halleonard.com**

Contact us:
**Hal Leonard**
7777 West Bluemound Road
Milwaukee, WI 53213
Email: info@halleonard.com

In Europe, contact:
**Hal Leonard Europe Limited**
42 Wigmore Street
Marylebone, London, W1U 2RN
Email: info@halleonardeurope.com

In Australia, contact:
**Hal Leonard Australia Pty. Ltd.**
4 Lentara Court
Cheltenham, Victoria, 3192 Australia
Email: info@halleonard.com.au

# Blue Eyes Crying in the Rain

## Words and Music by Fred Rose

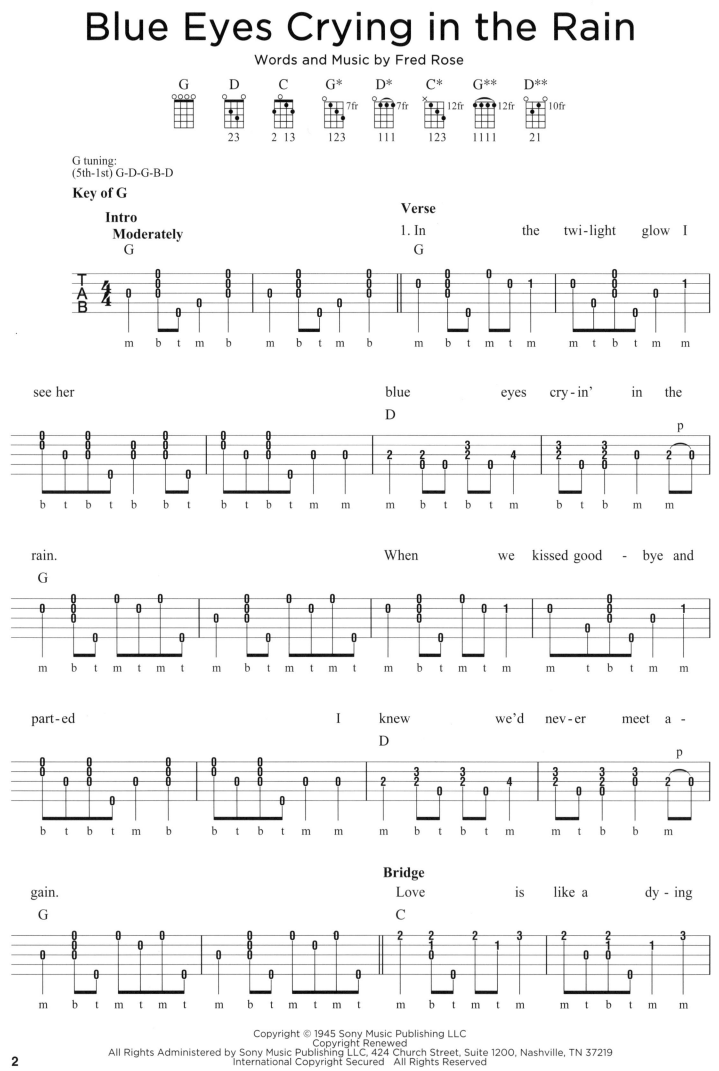

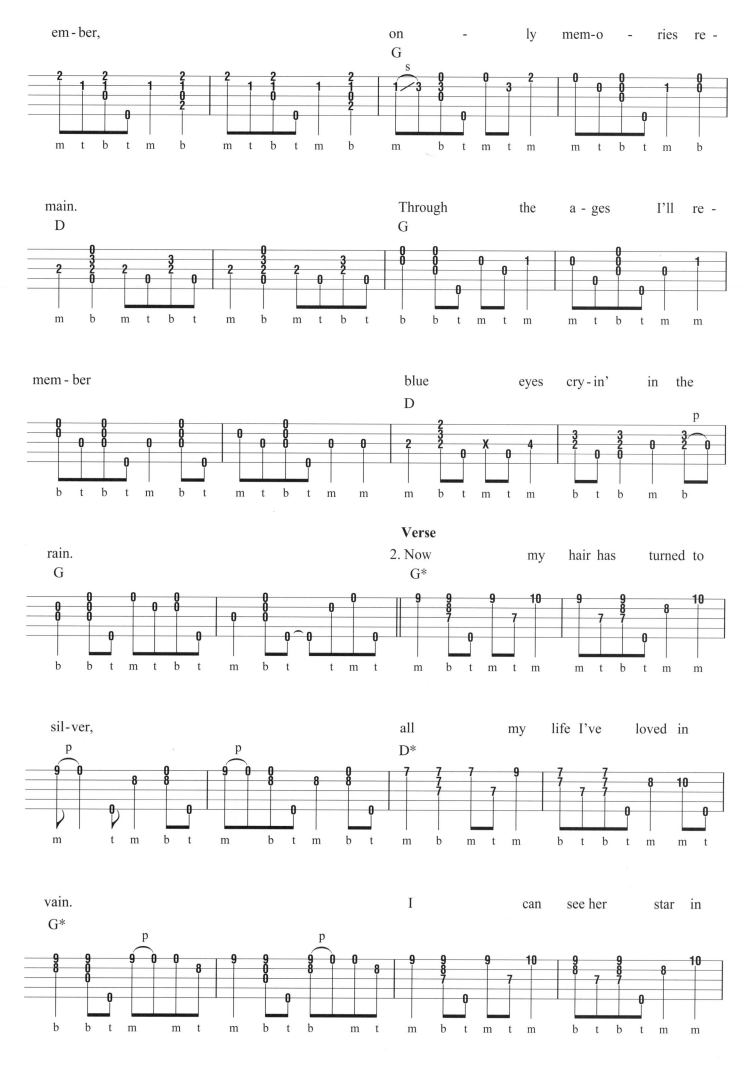

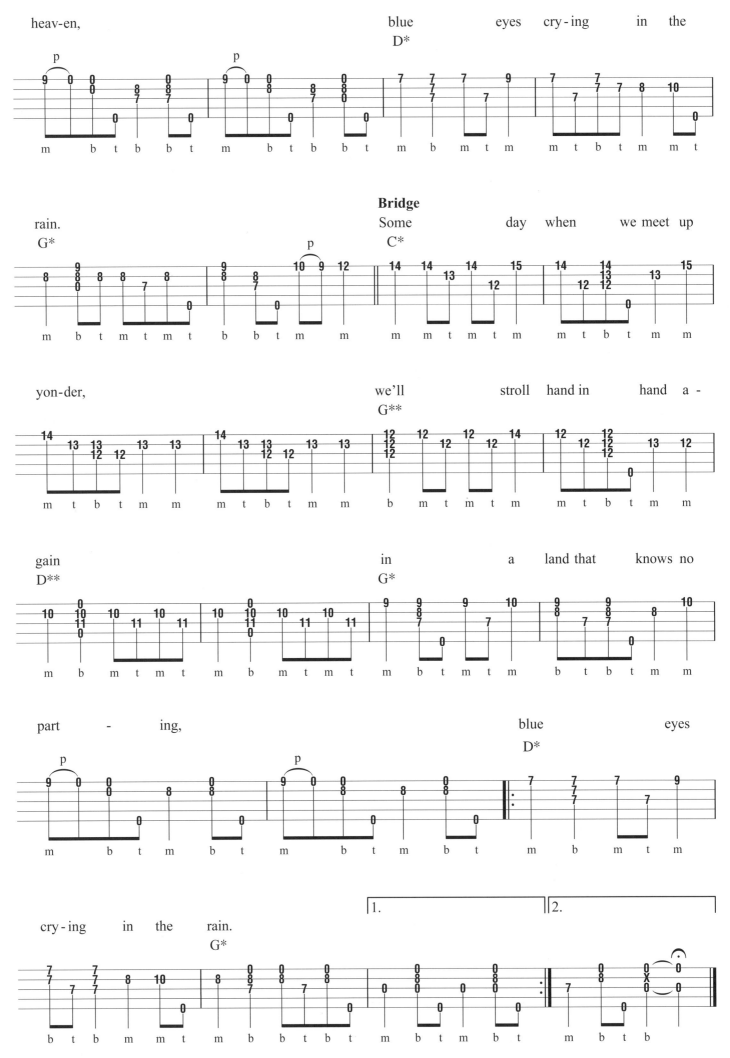

# El Paso

## Words and Music by Marty Robbins

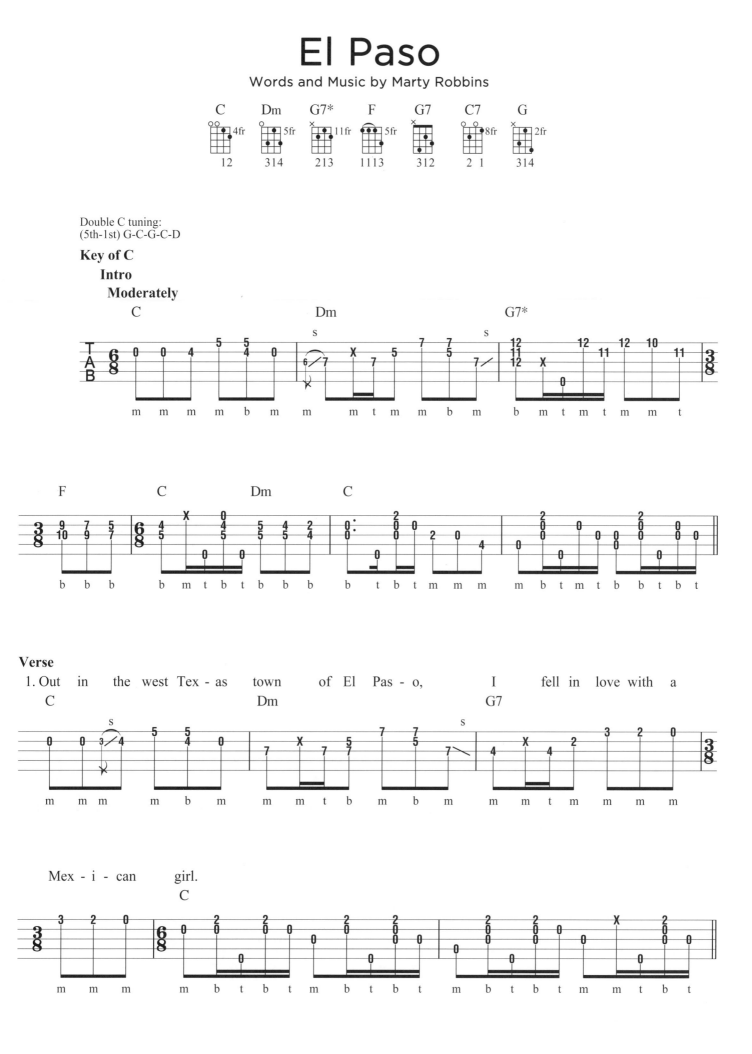

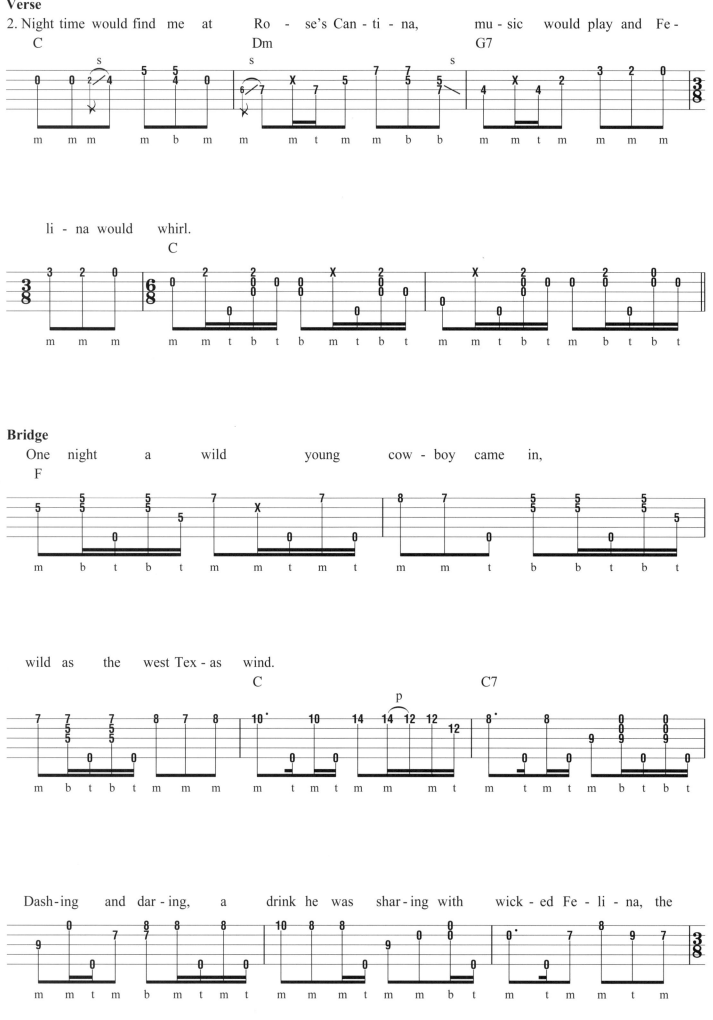

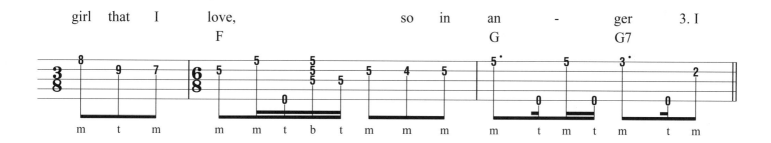

**Verse**

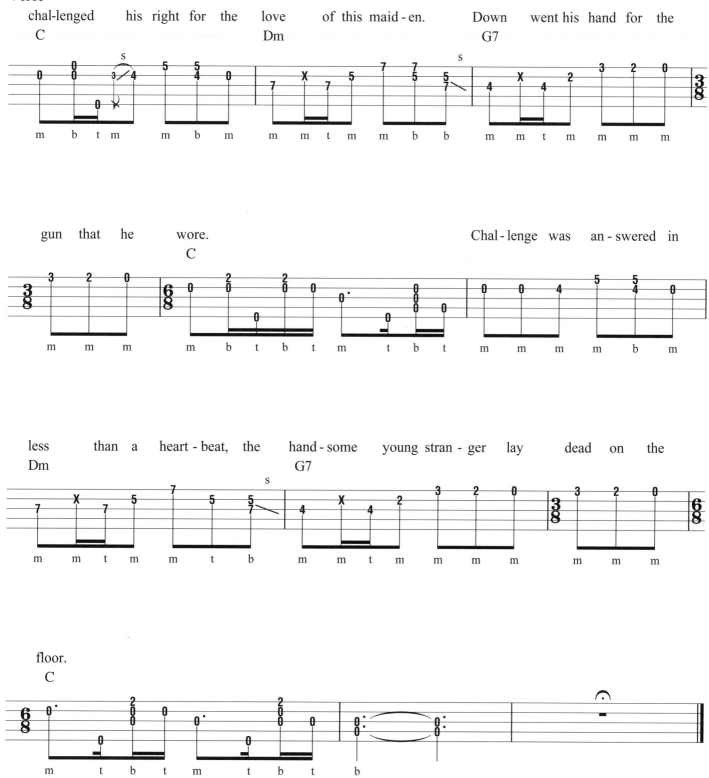

# Blue Yodel No. 1
## (T for Texas)

Words and Music by Jimmie Rodgers

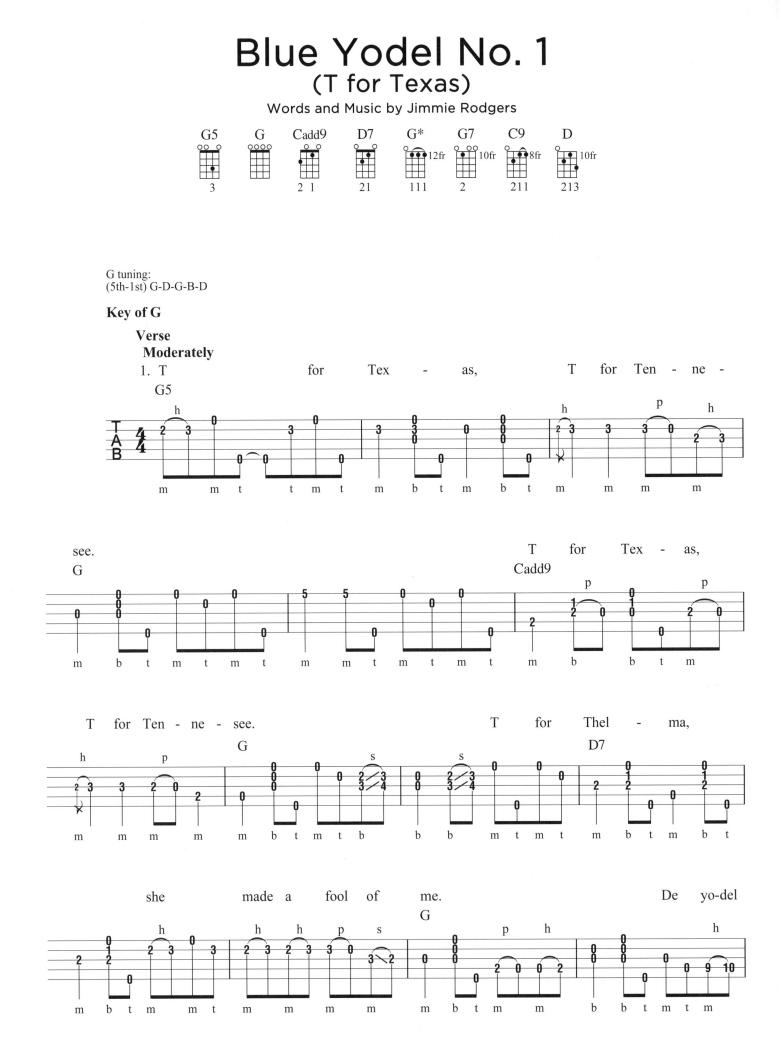

a - ee    a - ee    dee.

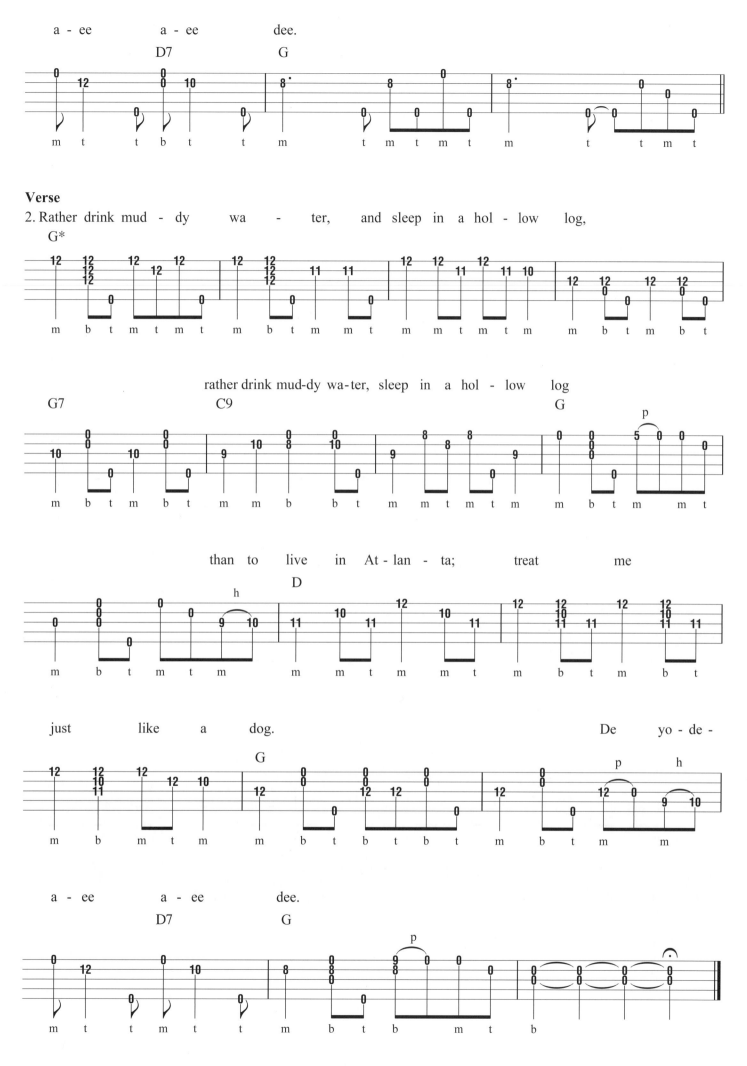

**Verse**

2. Rather drink mud - dy    wa    -    ter,    and sleep in a hol - low    log,

rather drink mud-dy wa-ter, sleep in a hol - low    log

than    to    live    in    At - lan - ta;    treat    me

just    like    a    dog.    De    yo - de -

a - ee    a - ee    dee.

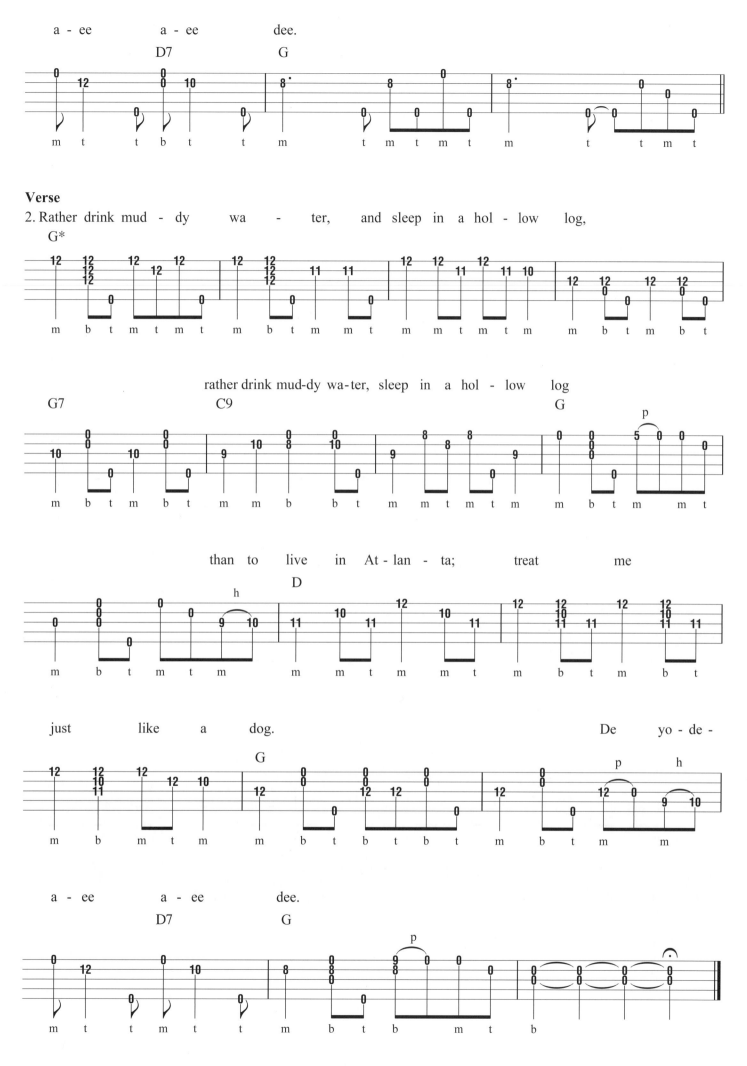

# Folsom Prison Blues

Words and Music by John R. Cash

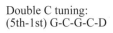

Double C tuning:
(5th–1st) G-C-G-C-D

**Key of C**

**Intro**
**Moderately**

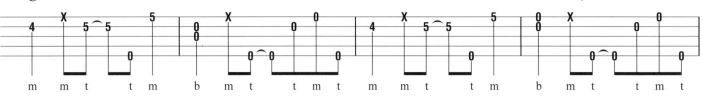

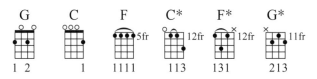

**Verse**

1. Hear the train a - com - in', roll - in' 'round the bend,

I ain't seen the sun - shine since I don't know when, 'cause I'm

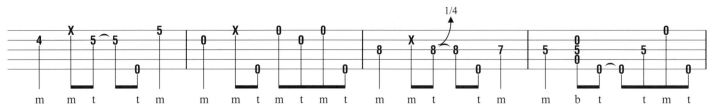

stuck at Fol - som Pri - son and time keeps drag - in'

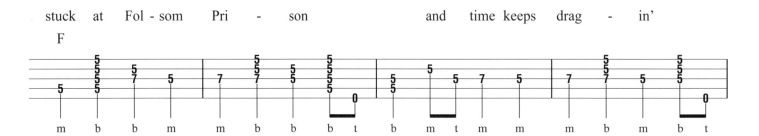

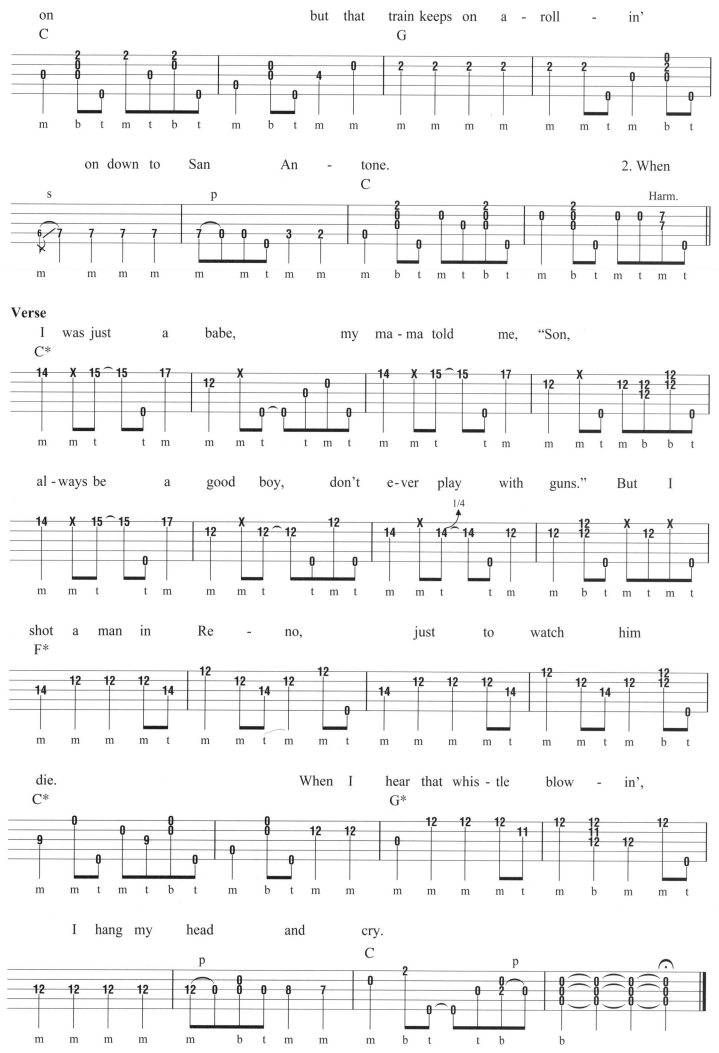

# Harper Valley P.T.A.

Words and Music by Tom T. Hall

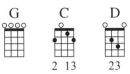

G tuning:
(5th-1st) G-D-G-B-D

**Key of G**

**Intro**

**Moderately**

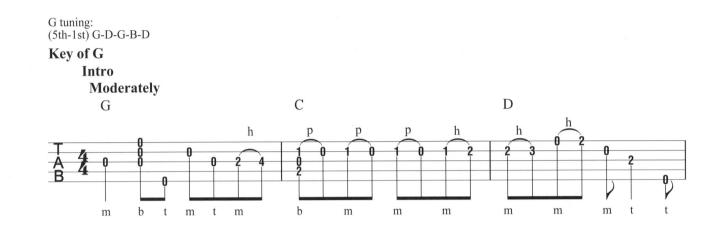

**Verse**

1. I want to    tell you all   a   sto - ry 'bout a

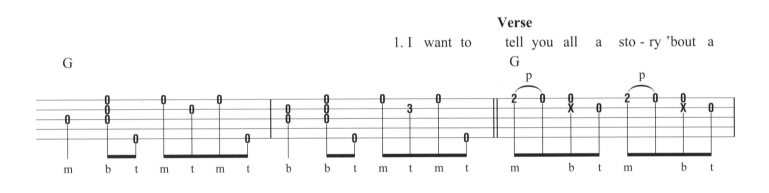

Har - per Val - ley wid - owed        wife                        who had a

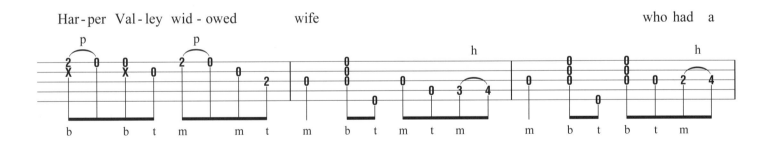

teen - age daugh-ter who at - tend-ed Har - per Val - ley Jun - ior High.

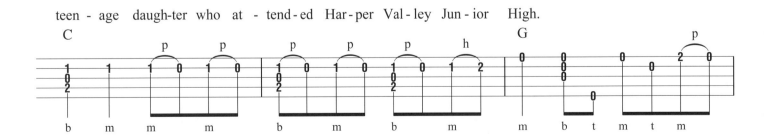

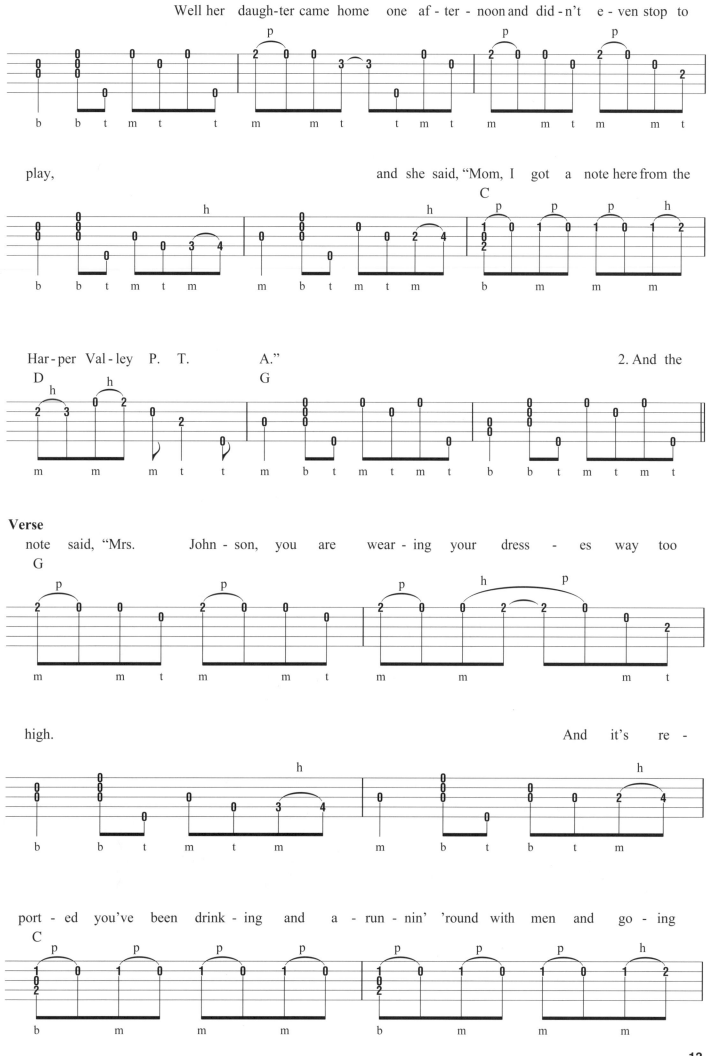

wild.                                                    And  we    don't be-lieve you ought to  be  a-

bring - ing    up    your    lit - tle    girl    this    way."

And    it    was    signed         by    the    sec - re - tar - y,

Har - per  Val - ley  P.  T.              A.

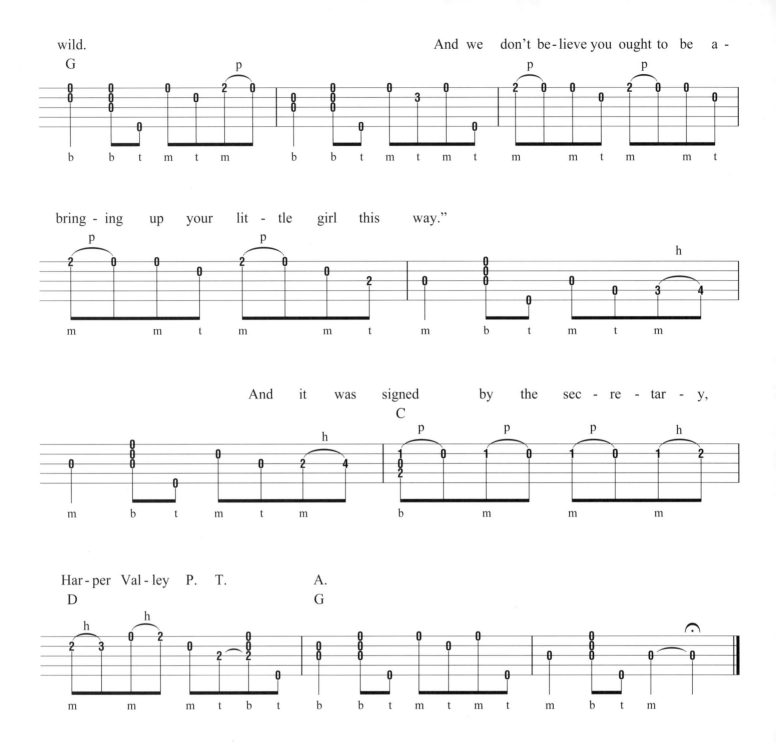

# Hey, Good Lookin'

Words and Music by Hank Williams

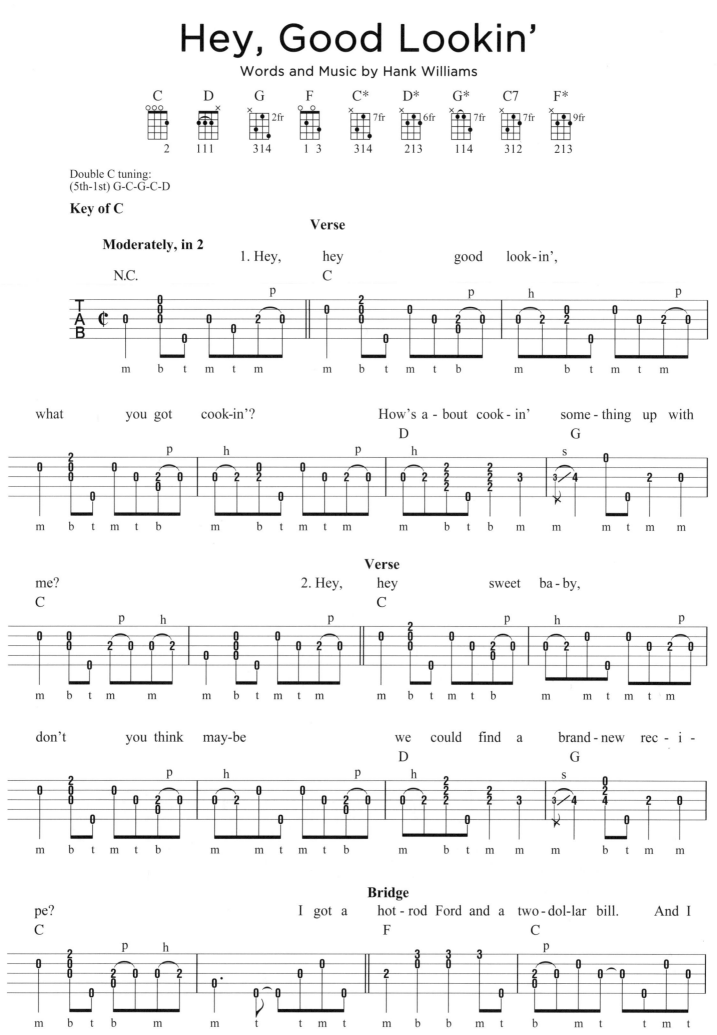

15

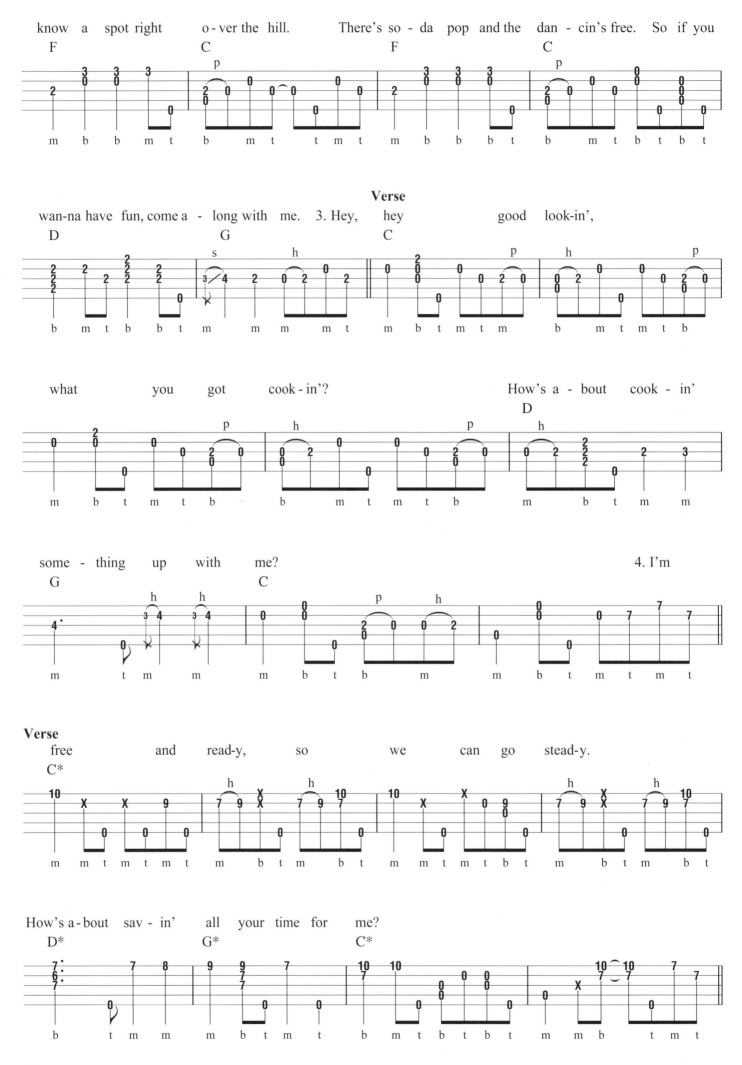

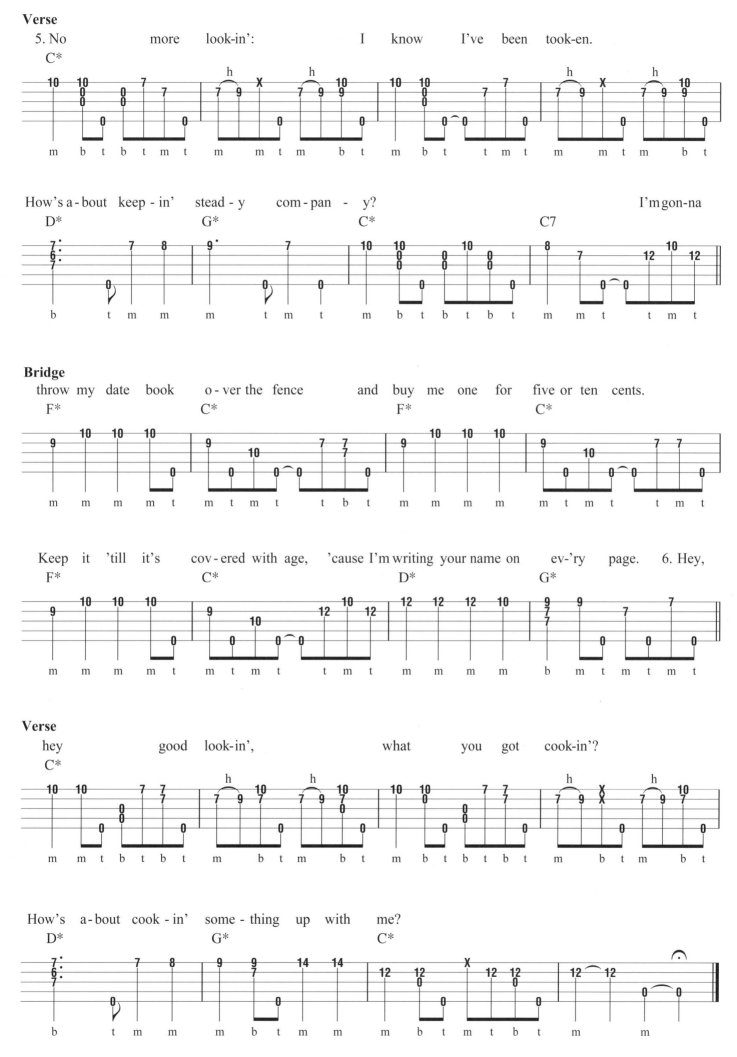

# Hickory Wind

Words and Music by Gram Parsons and Bob Buchanan

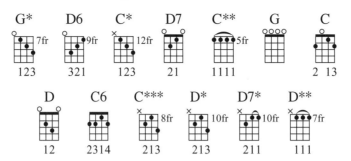

G tuning:
(5th-1st) G-D-G-B-D

**Key of G**

**Intro**

**Moderately**

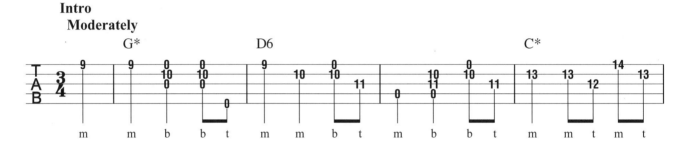

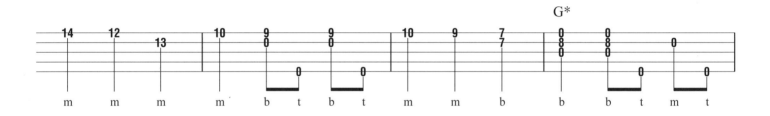

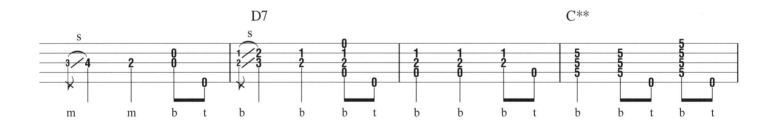

1. In

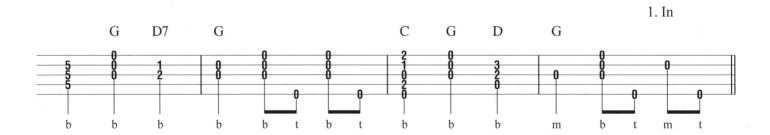

**Verse**

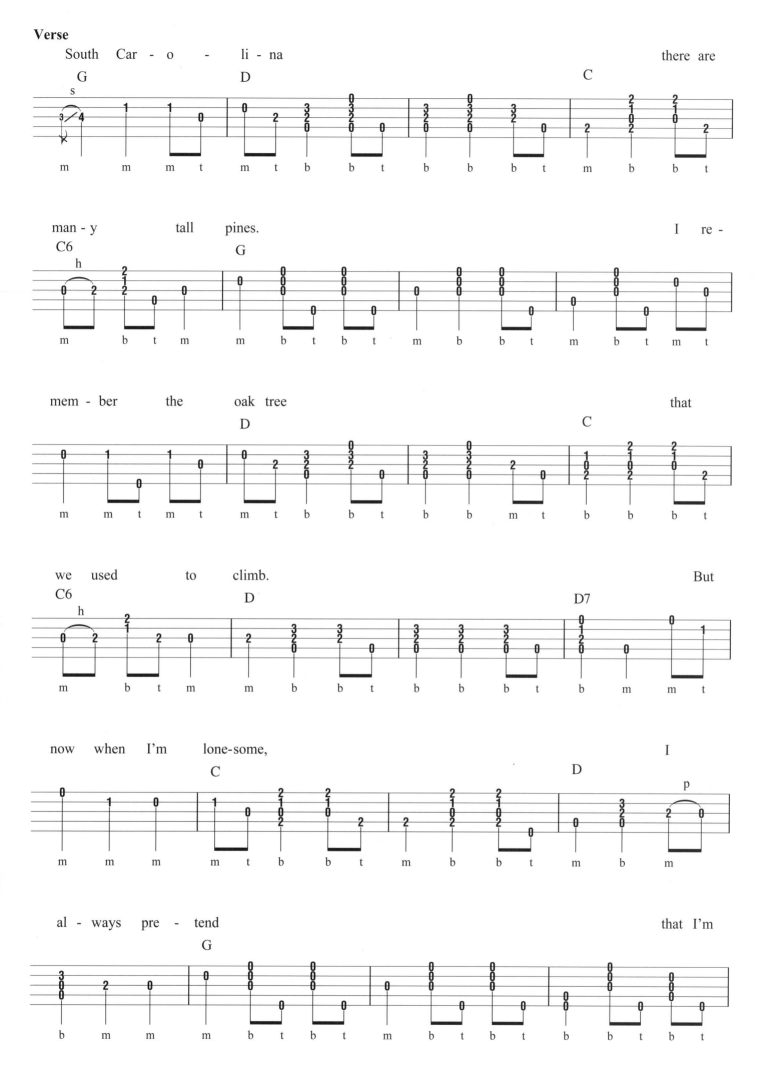

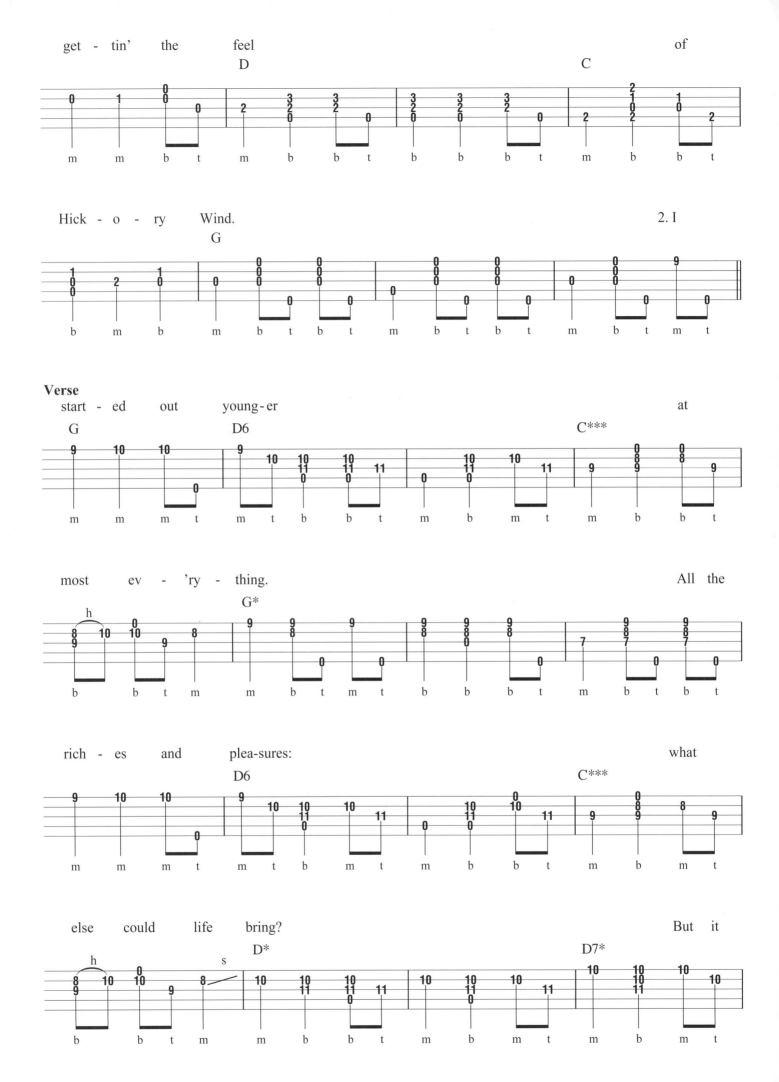

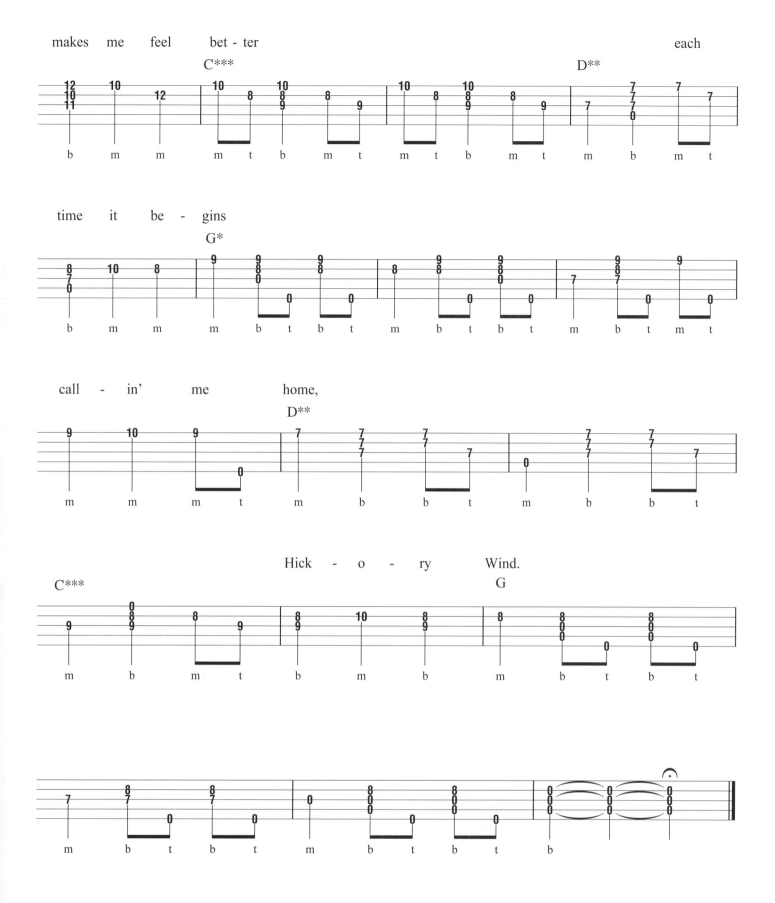

# I Walk the Line

Words and Music by John R. Cash

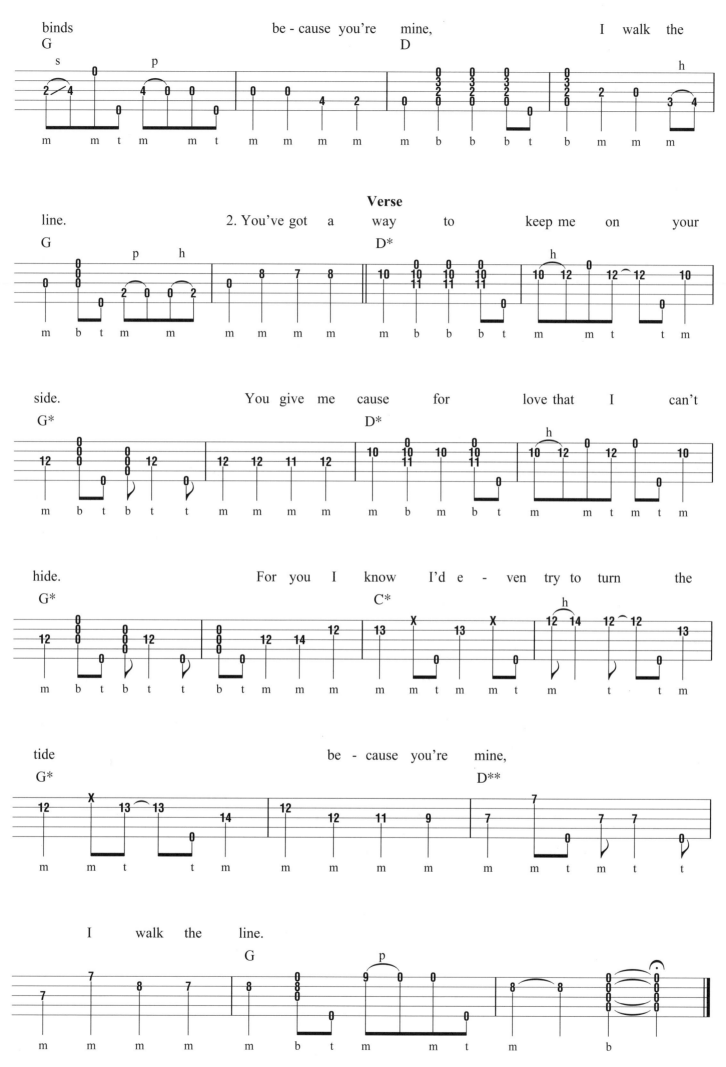

# I Will Always Love You

Words and Music by Dolly Parton

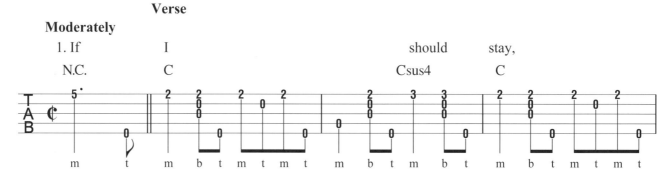

Double C tuning:
(5th-1st) G-C-G-C-D

**Key of C**

**Verse**

**Moderately**

1. If        I                       should      stay,
N.C.        C                                    Csus4        C

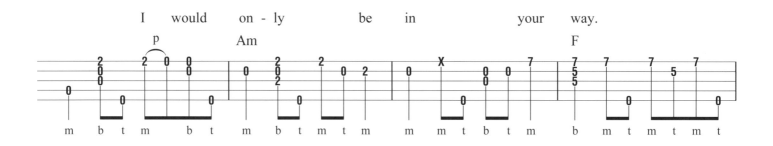

I     would     on - ly          be     in          your     way.
                    p          Am                                    F

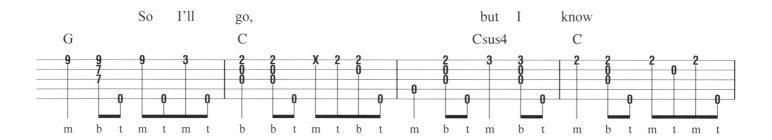

So        I'll        go,                          but        I        know
G                           C                                    Csus4        C

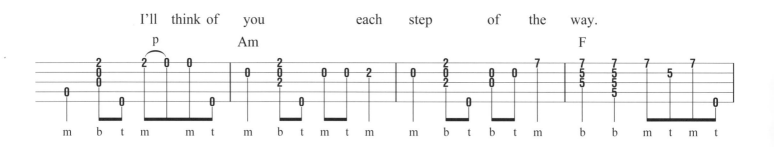

I'll     think     of     you          each     step     of     the     way.
                    p          Am                                            F

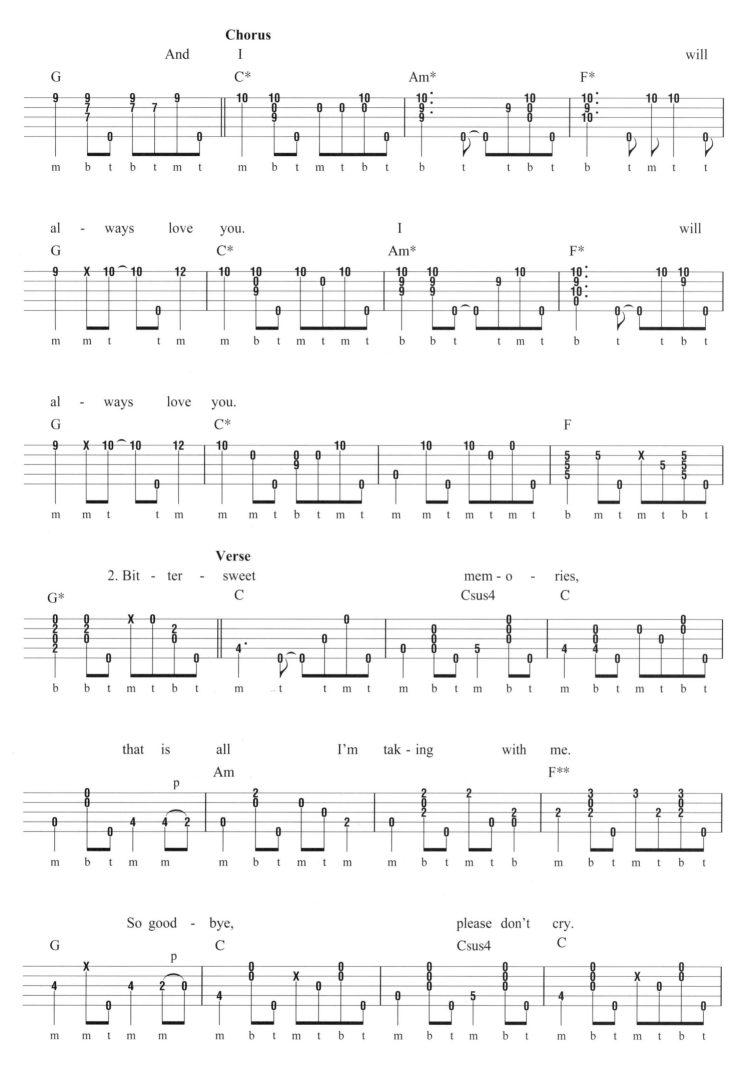

We    both    know                    I'm    not          what    you

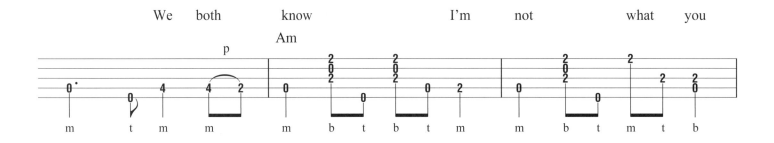

need.                                    And          I,

**Chorus**

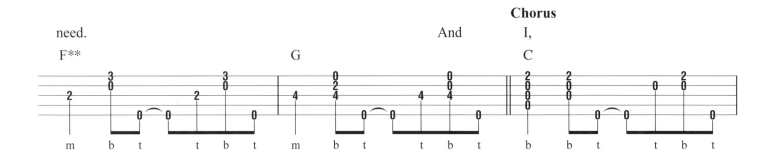

I                                    will          al  -  ways    love,

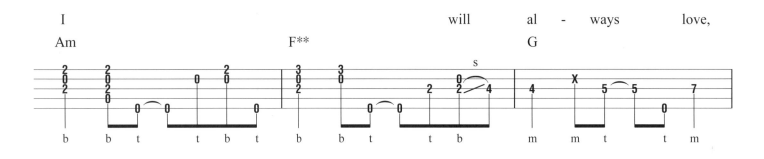

I,                          I                                    will

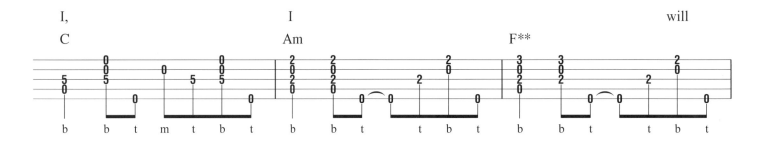

al  -  ways    love    you.

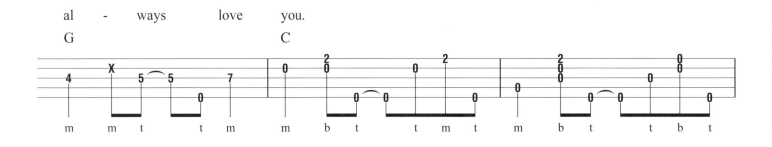

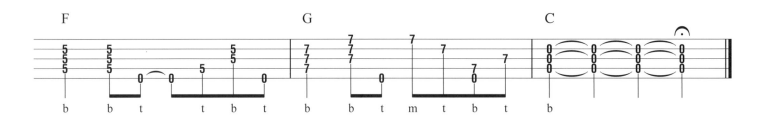

# If I Had a Boat

## Words and Music by Lyle Lovett

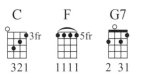

Open C tuning:
(5th-1st) G-C-G-C-E

**Key of C**

  **Intro**

  **Moderately**

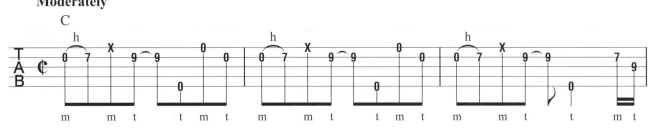

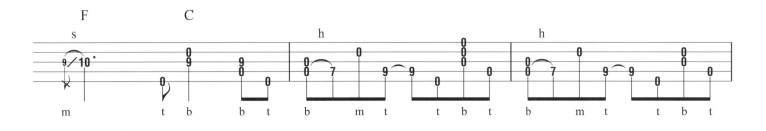

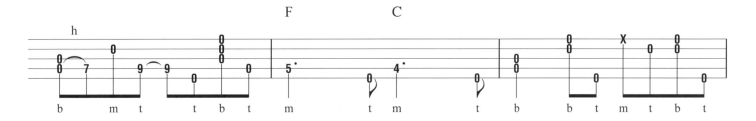

**𝄋 Chorus**

If I had a boat,      I'd

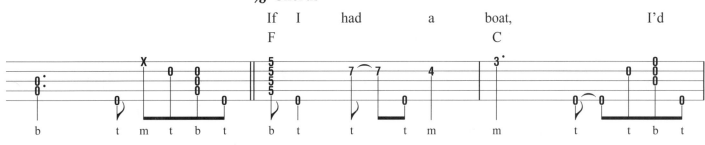

go out on the o - cean.      If I had a

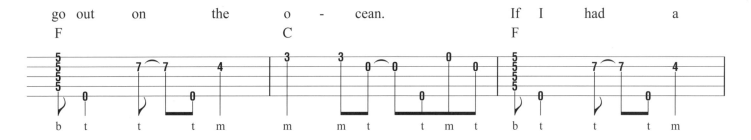

Copyright © 1987 Michael H. Goldsen, Inc. and Lyle Lovett
All Rights Reserved   Used by Permission

27

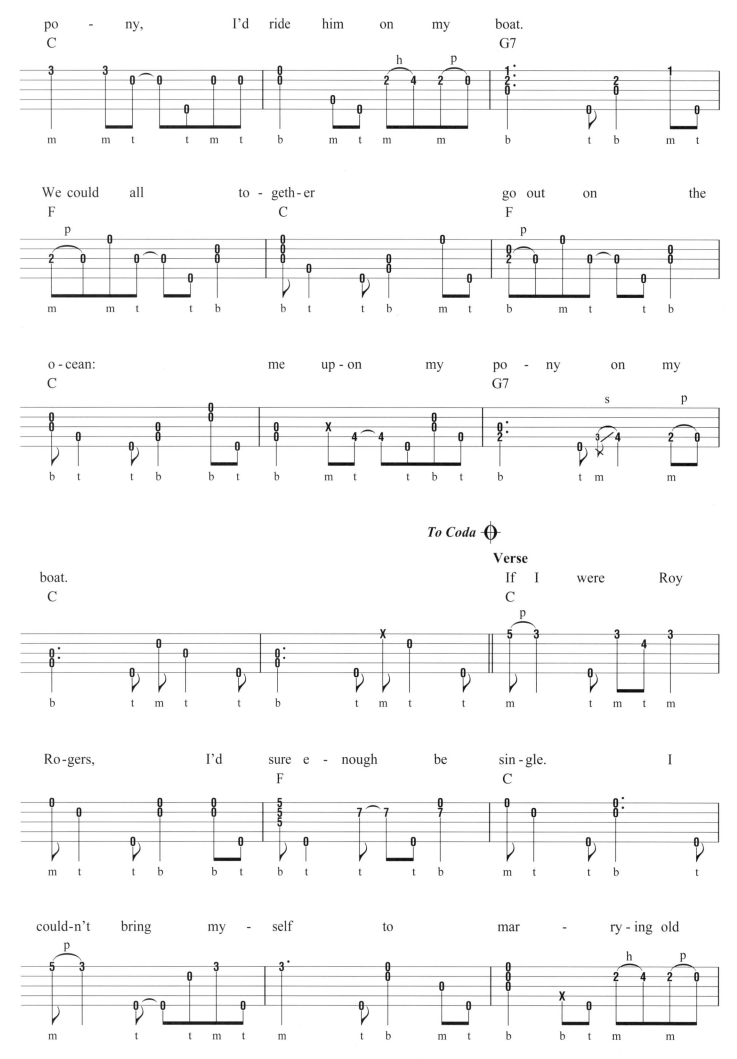

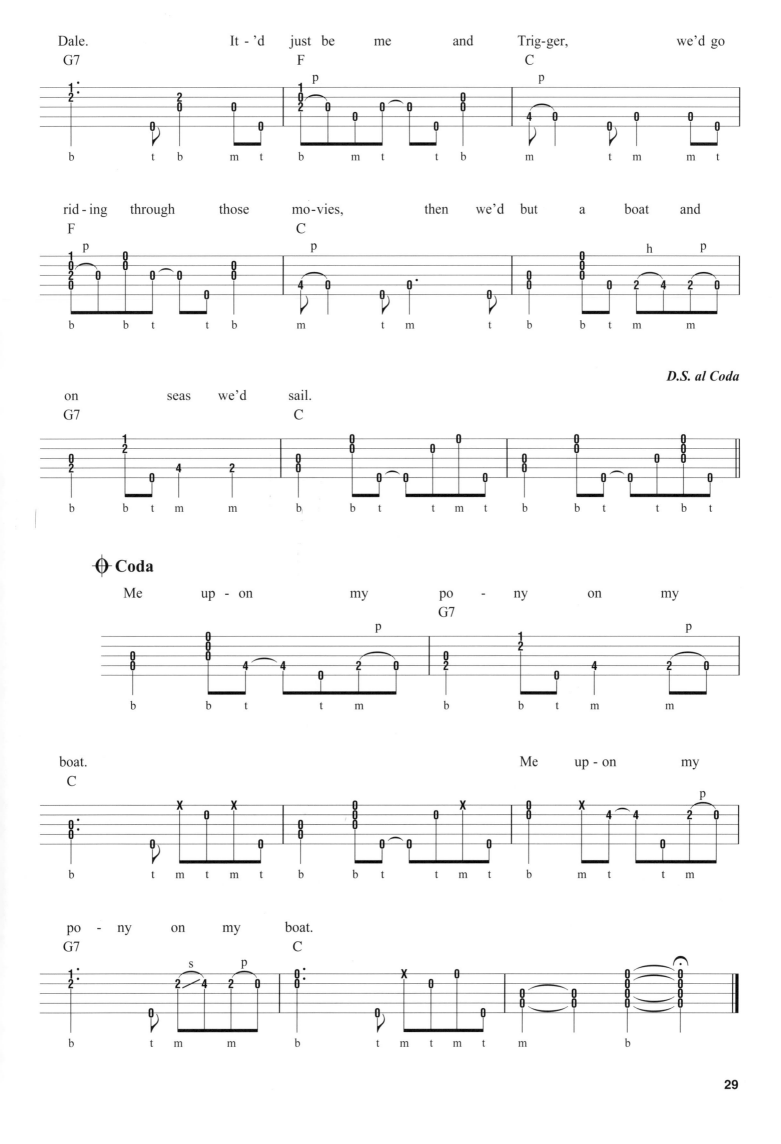

*D.S. al Coda*

**Coda**

# Jambalaya
## (On the Bayou)

Words and Music by Hank Williams

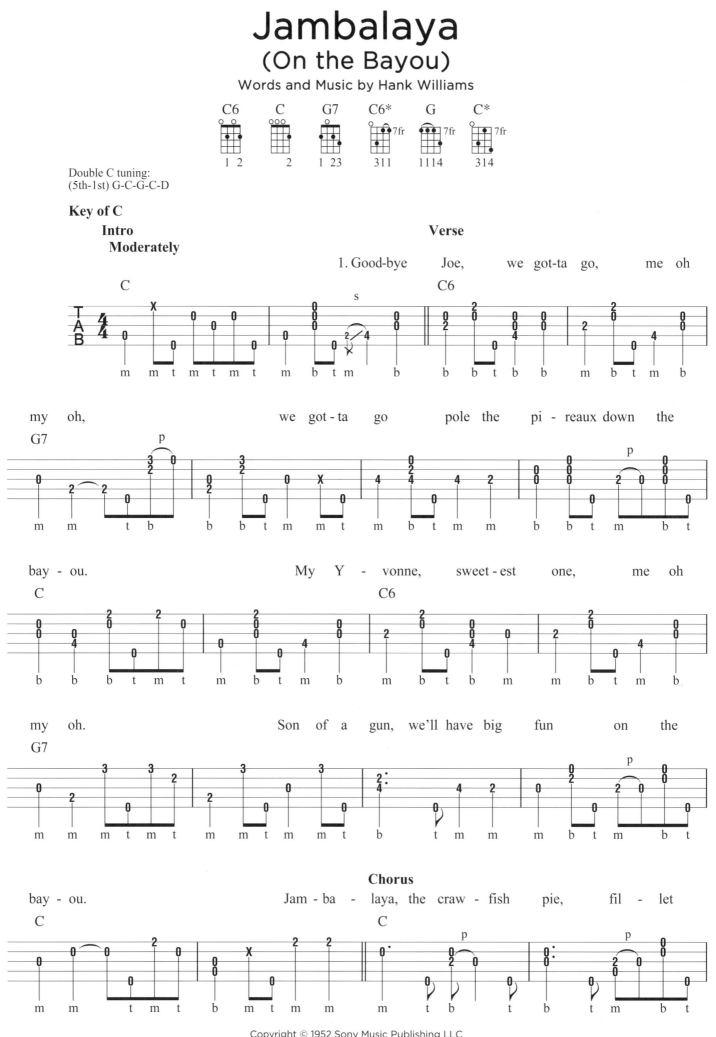

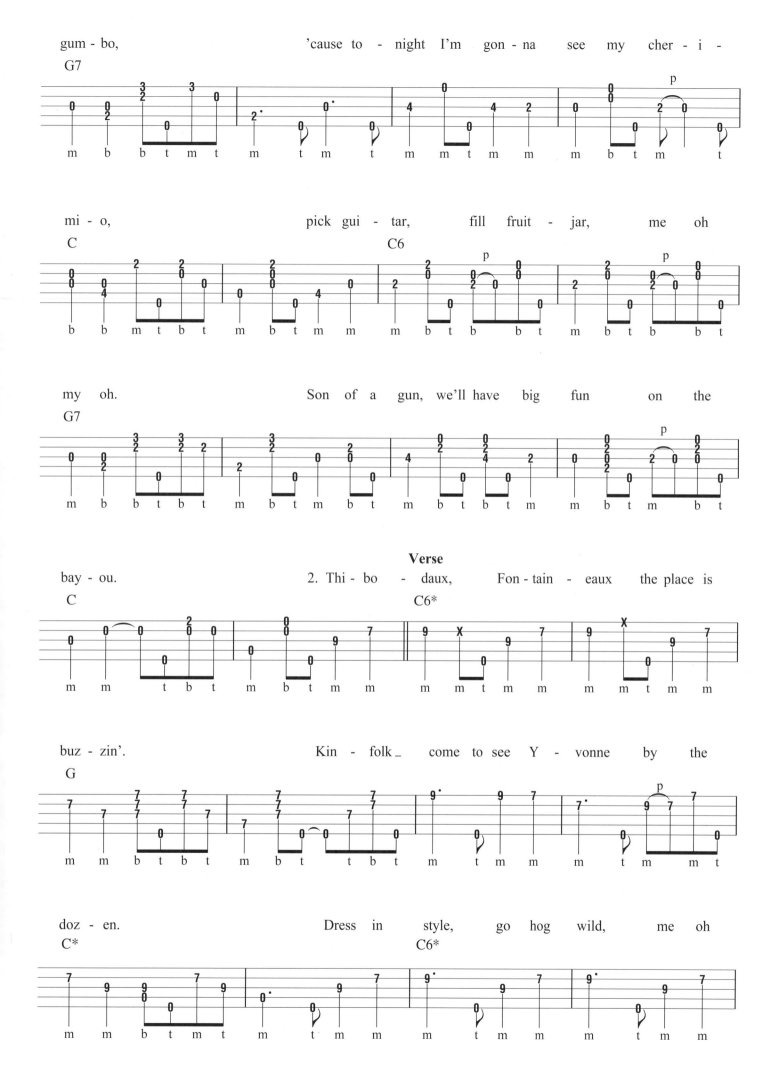

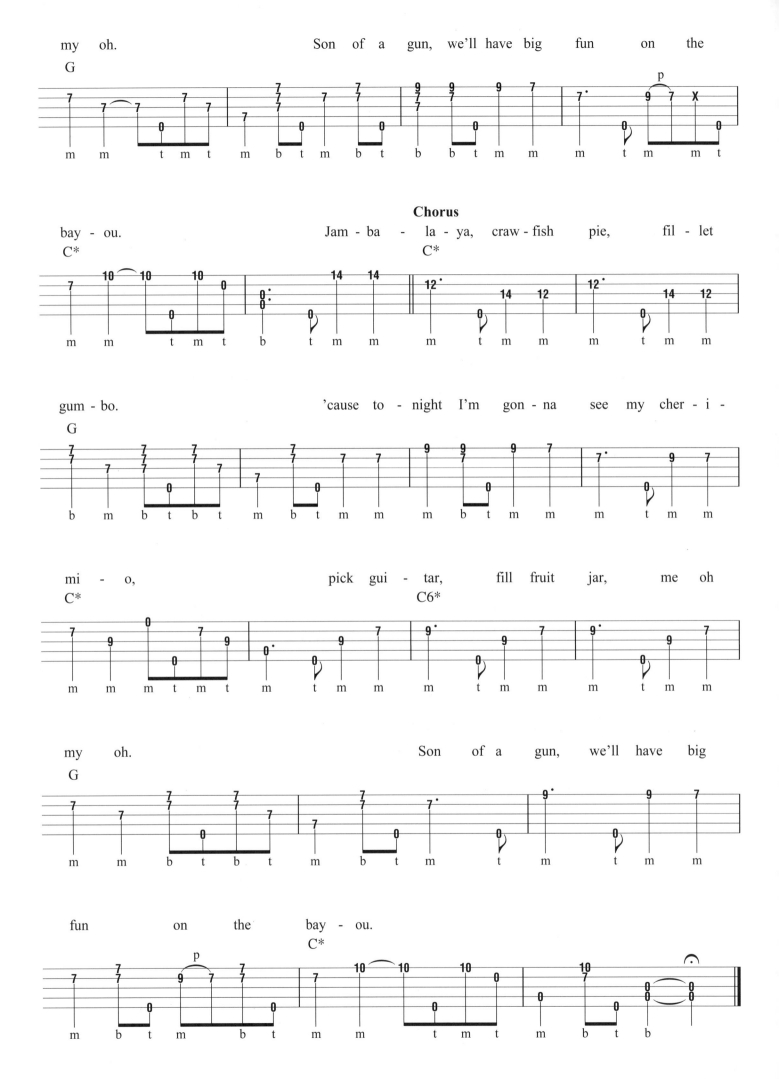

# Jolene

### Words and Music by Dolly Parton

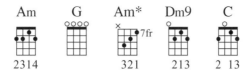

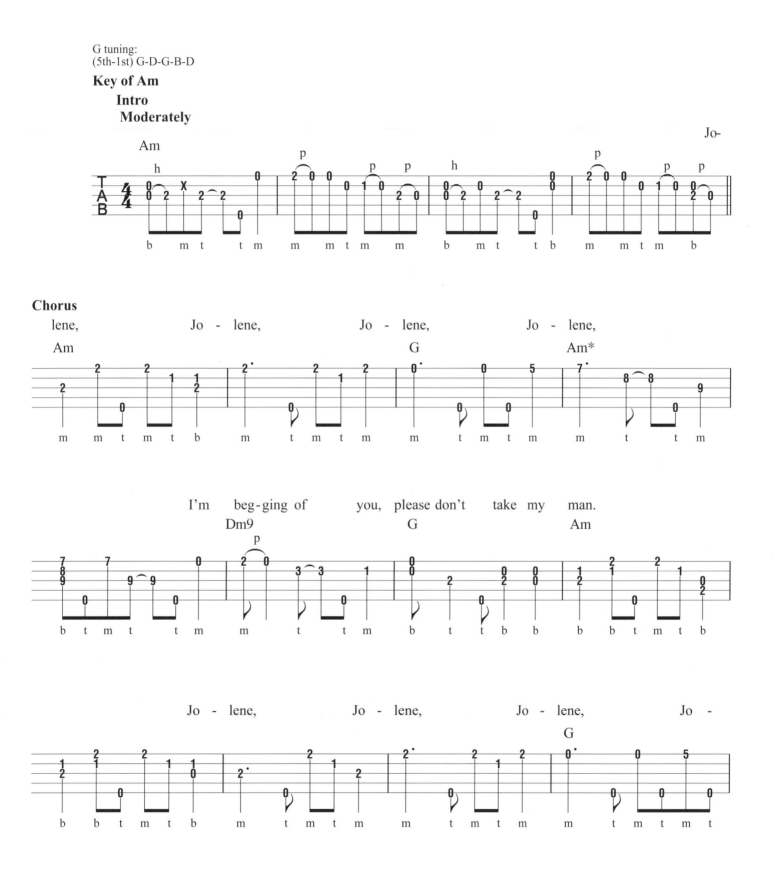

lene, please don't take him just be - cause you

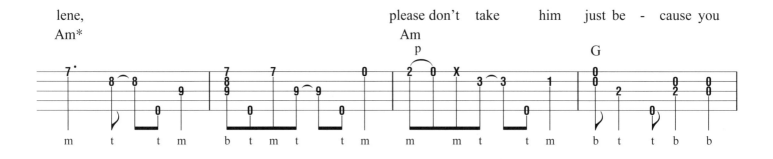

can. Your beau - ty is be - yond com-pare with

**Verse**

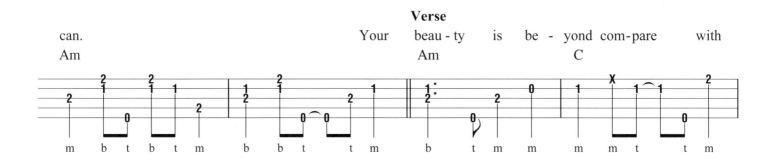

flam - ing locks of au - burn hair, with iv - 'ry skin and eyes of em - 'rald

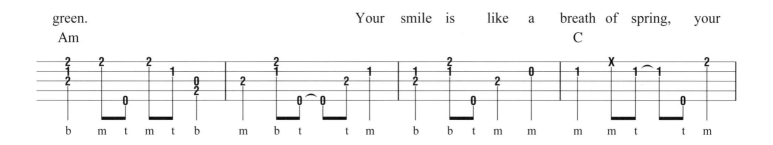

green. Your smile is like a breath of spring, your

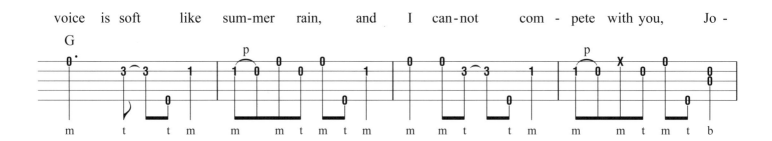

voice is soft like sum-mer rain, and I can-not com - pete with you, Jo -

**Chorus**

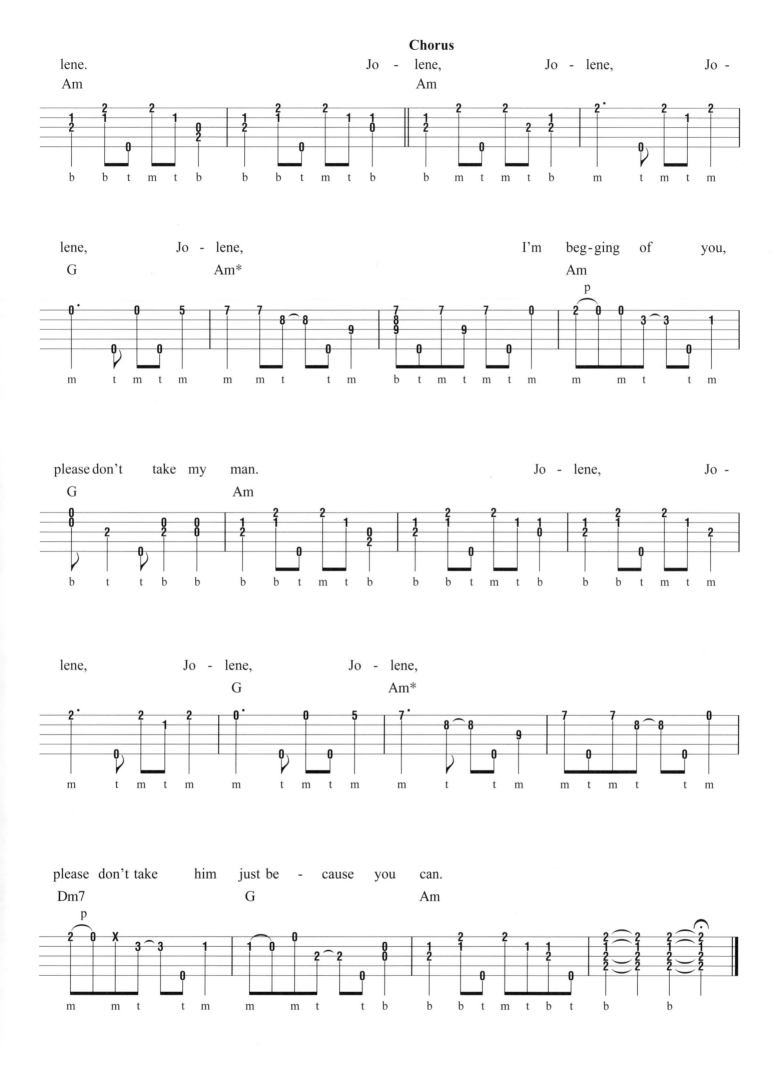

# The Long Black Veil

Words and Music by Marijohn Wilkin and Danny Dill

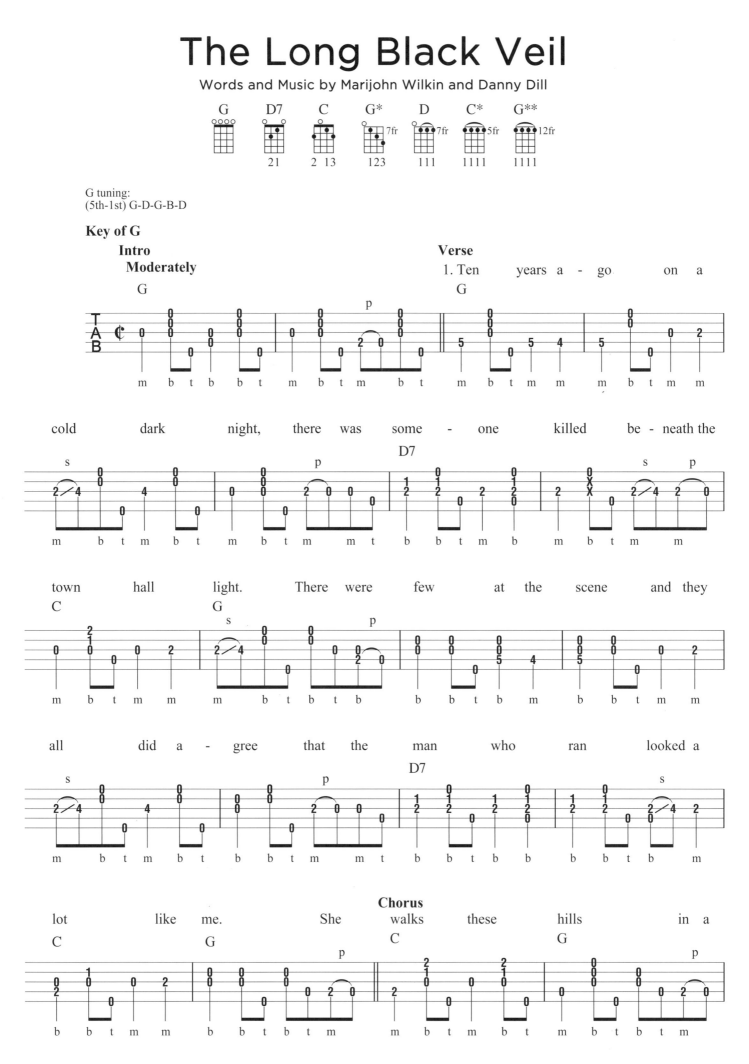

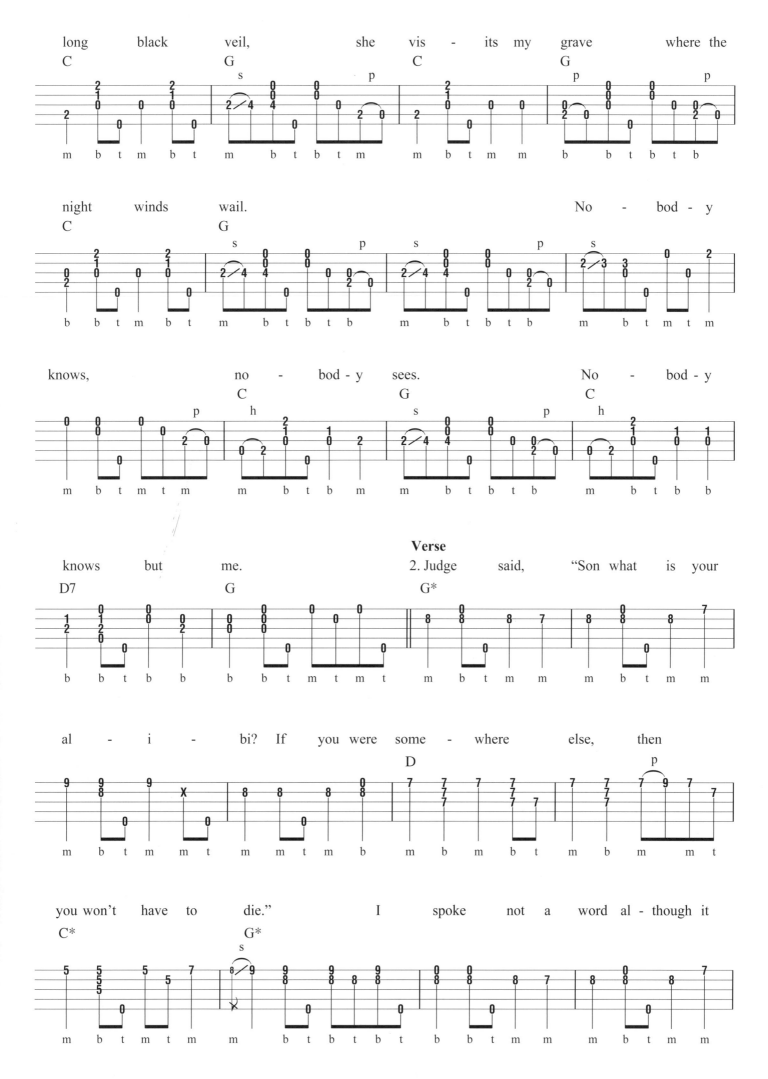

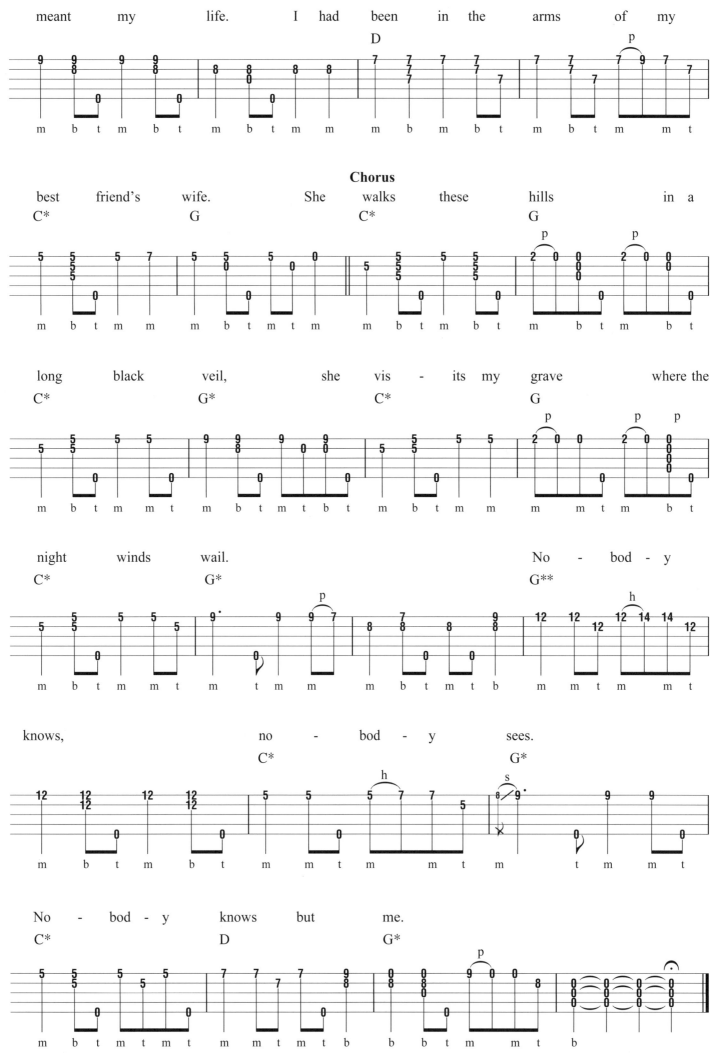

# Pancho and Lefty

Words and Music by Townes Van Zandt

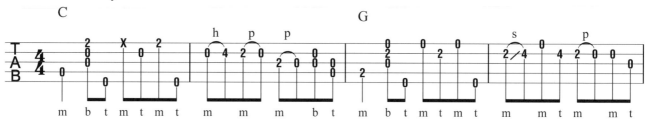

Double C tuning:
(5th-1st) G-C-G-C-D

**Key of C**

**Intro**

**Moderately**

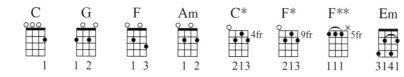

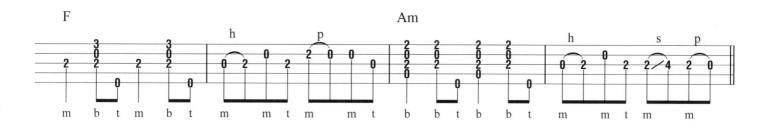

**Verse**

1. Liv - in' on the road, my friend, was gon - na keep us
2. *See additional lyrics*

free and clean. But now you wear your skin like i - ron and your

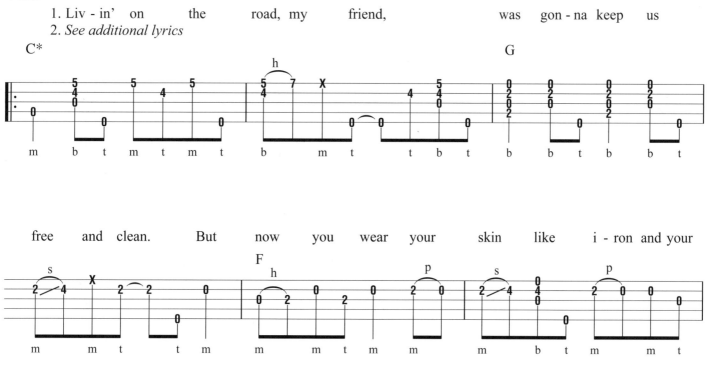

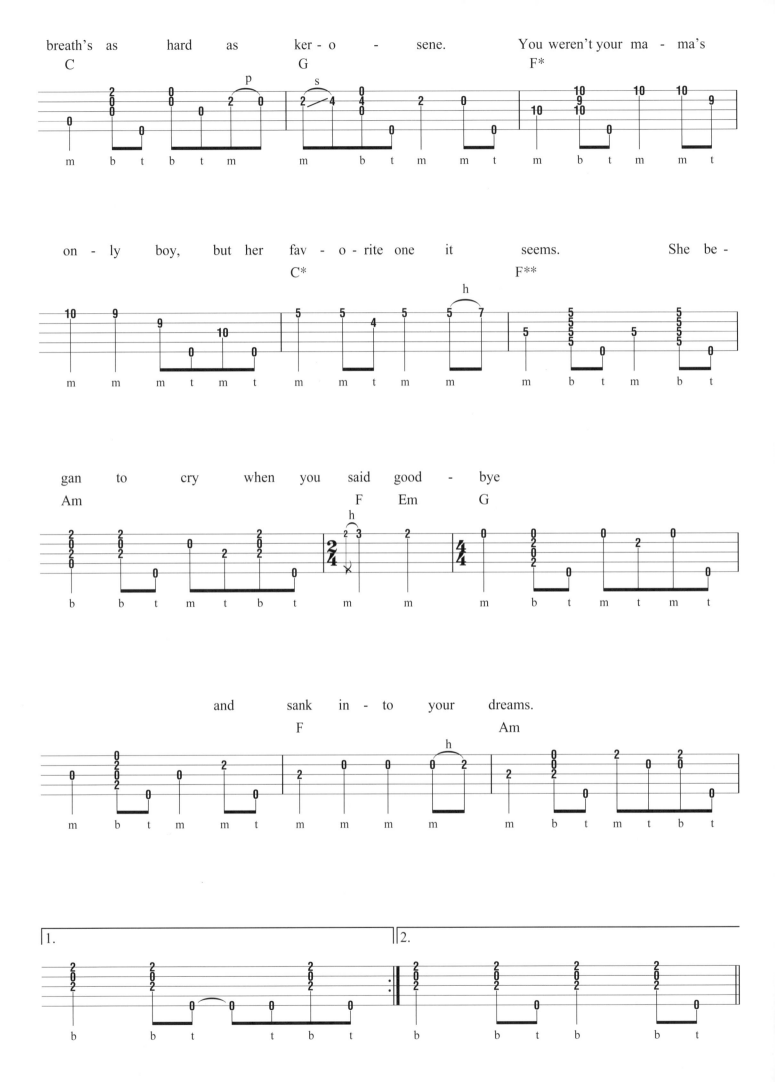

**Chorus**

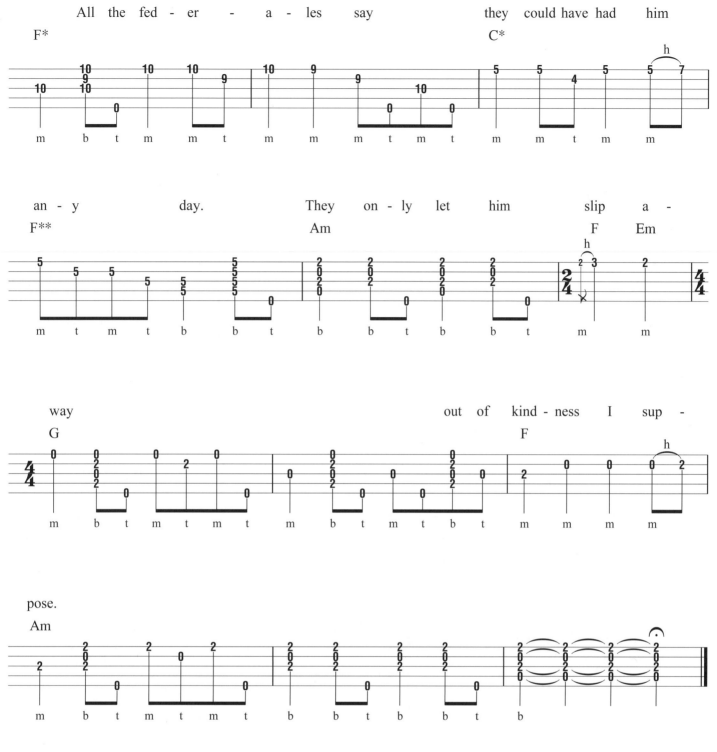

*Additional Lyrics*

2. Pancho was a bandit, boys,
   His horse was fast as polished steel,
   Wore his gun outside his pants
   For all the honest world to feel.
   Pancho met his match you know
   On the deserts down in Mexico.
   Nobody heard his dying words.
   That's the way it goes.

# Ode to Billy Joe

Words and Music by Bobbie Gentry

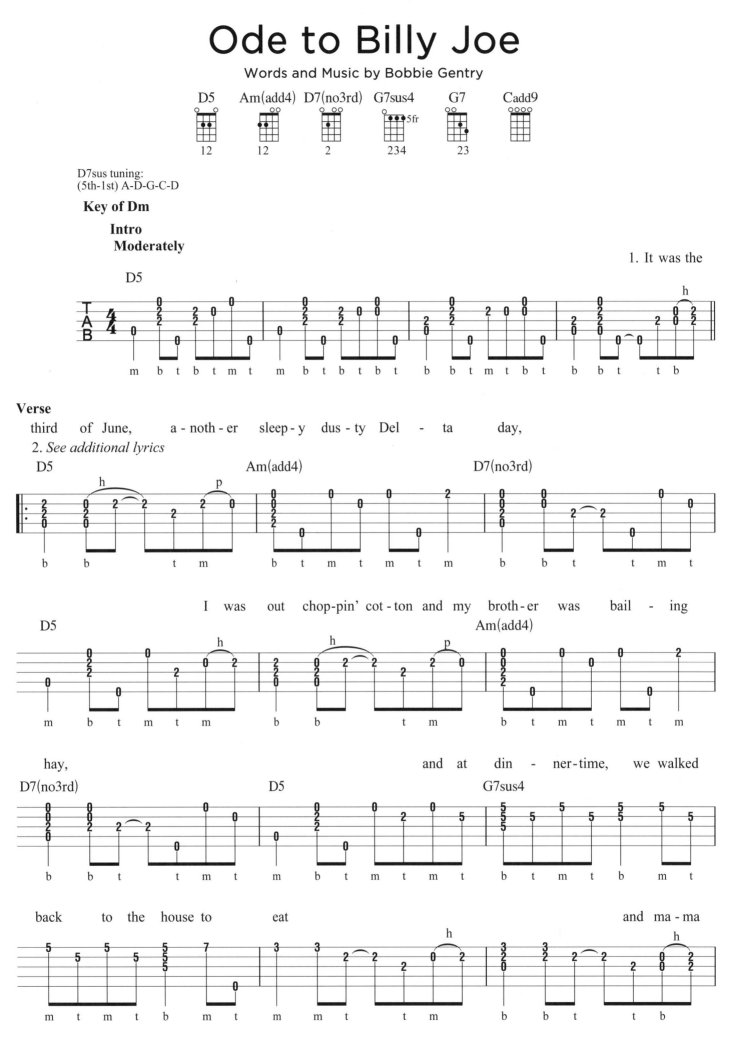

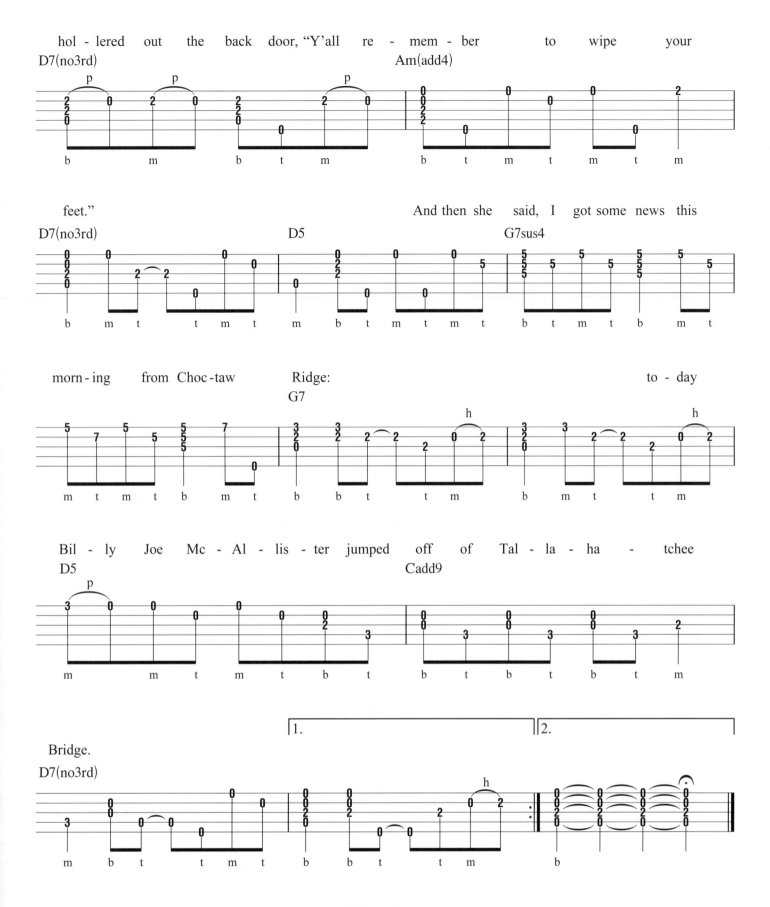

*Additional Lyrics*

2. And papa said to mama, as he passed around the blackeyed peas,
   "Well, Billy Joe never had a lick of sense; pass the biscuits, please.
   There's five more acres in the lower forty I've got to plow."
   And mama said it was shame about Billy Joe, anyhow.
   Seems like nothin' ever comes to no good up on Choctaw Ridge
   And now Billy Joe McAllister's jumped off the Tallahatchie Bridge.

# Okie from Muskogee

Words and Music by Merle Haggard and Roy Edward Burris

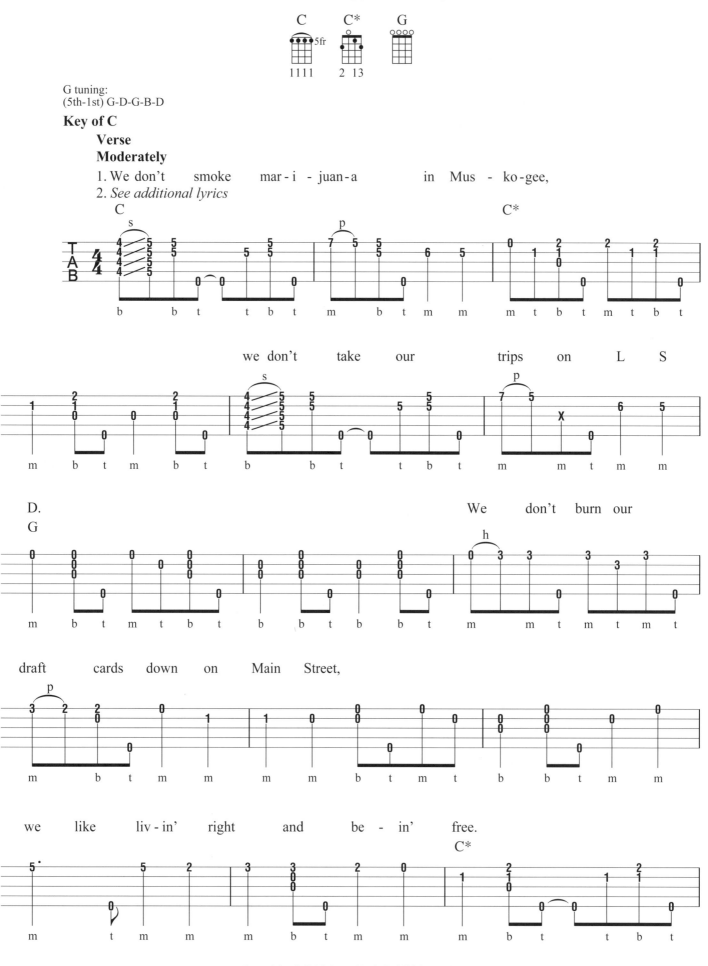

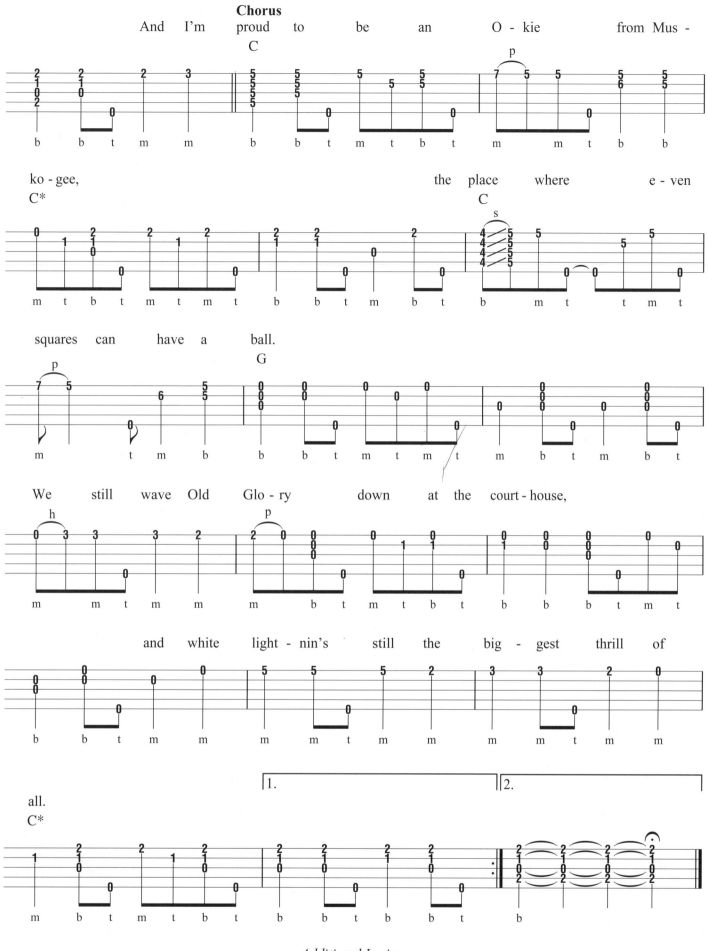

*Additional Lyrics*

2. We don't make a party out of lovin',
   We like holdin' hands and pitchin' woo.
   We don't let our hair grow long and shaggy
   Like the hippies out in San Francisco do.

# Seven Year Ache

Words and Music by Rosanne Cash

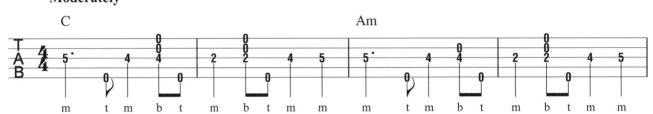

Double C tuning:
(5th-1st) G-C-G-C-D

**Key of C**

**Intro**
**Moderately**

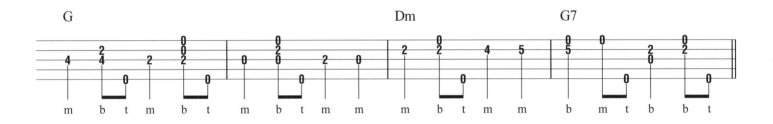

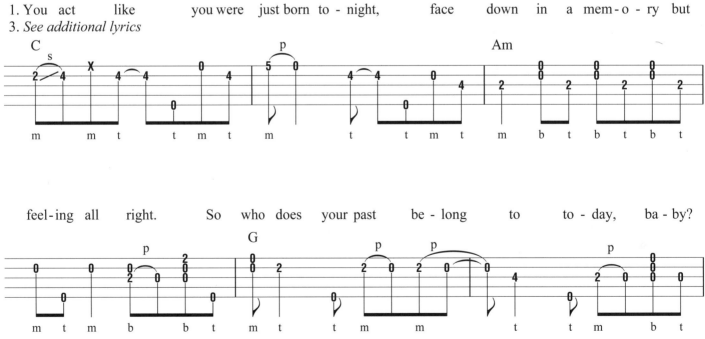

𝄋 **Verse**

1. You act like you were just born to - night, face down in a mem-o-ry but
3. *See additional lyrics*

feel-ing all right. So who does your past be - long to to - day, ba - by?

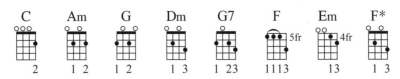

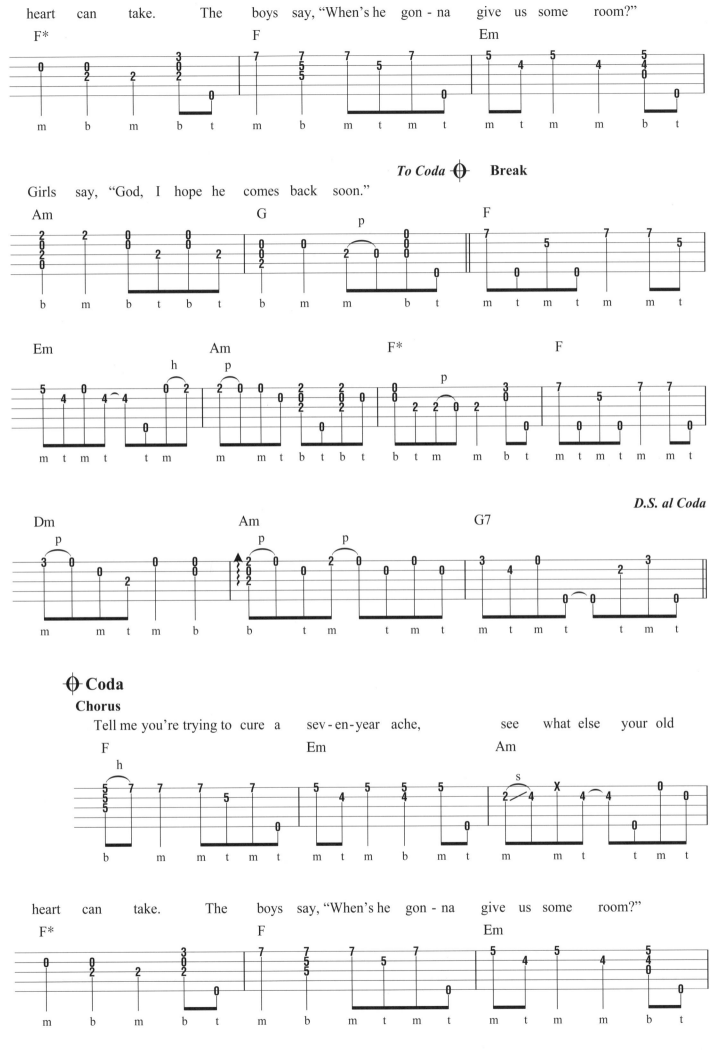

Girls     say,     "God,     I     hope     he     comes     back     soon."

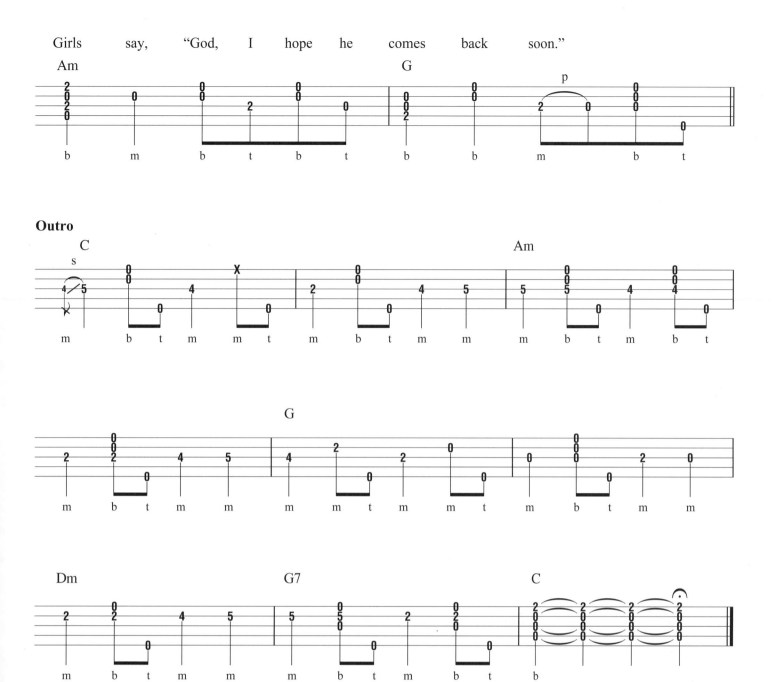

**Outro**

*Additional Lyrics*

3. Everybody's talking but you don't hear a thing,
   You're still uptown on your downhill swing.
   Boulevard's empty, why don't you come around?
   Baby, what is so great about sleeping downtown?

4. Splitting your dice to be someone you're not,
   You say you're looking for something you might've forgot.
   Don't bother calling to say you're leaving alone
   'Cause there's a fool on every corner when you're trying to get home.

# Waiting for a Train

Words and Music by Jimmie Rodgers

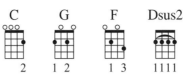

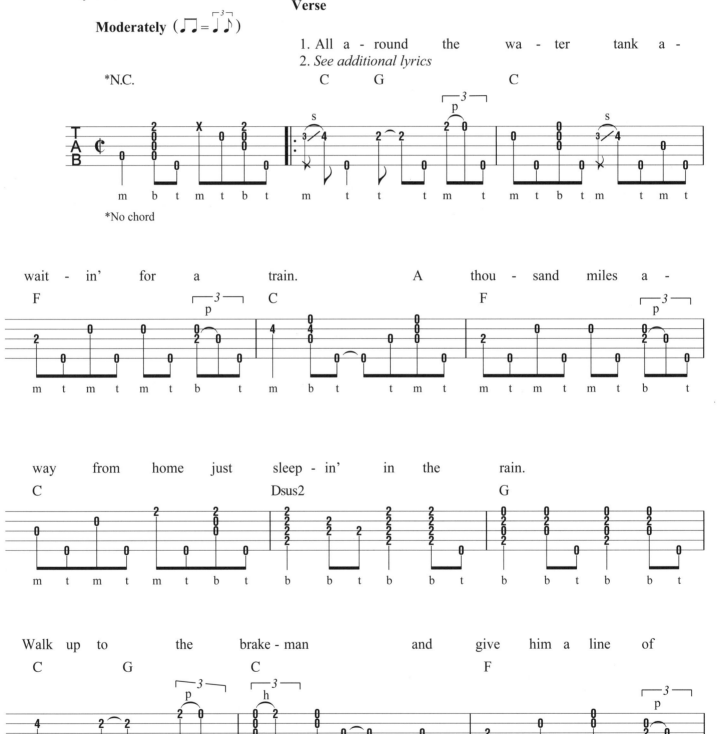

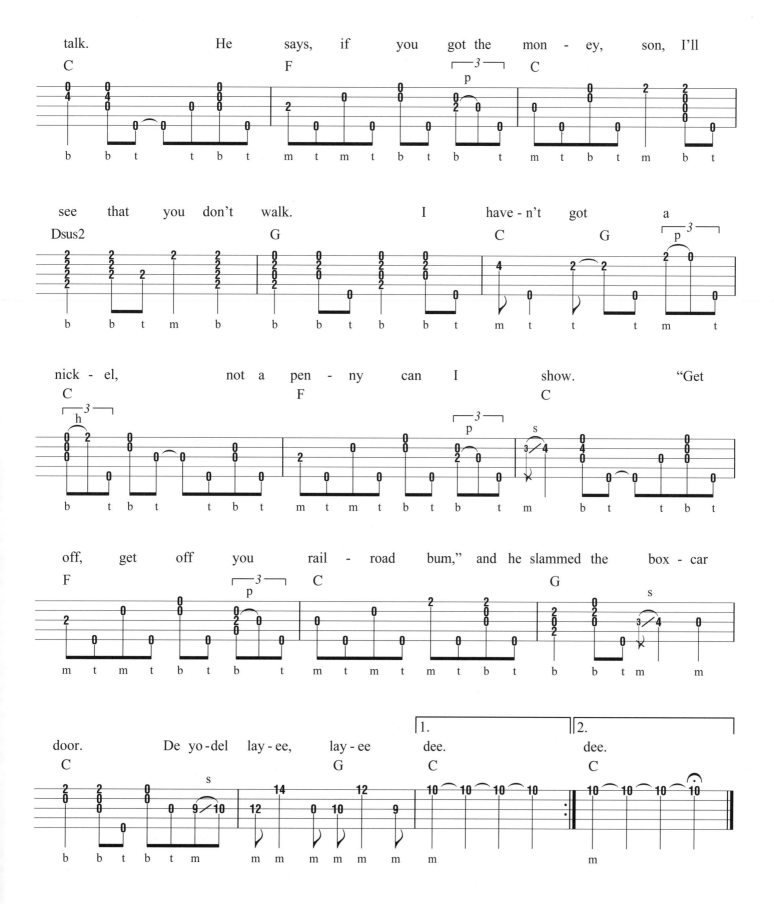

*Additional Lyrics*

2. He put me off in Texas, a state I dearly love.
   The wide open spaces all around me,
   The moon and stars up above.
   Nobody seems to want me or lend me a helping hand.
   I'm on my way from Frisco, going back to Dixie Land.
   Though my pocketbook is empty and my heart is full of pain,
   I'm a thousand miles away from home, just a-waiting for a train.
   De yodel lay-ee, lay-ee, dee.

# When I Call Your Name

Words and Music by Vince Gill and Tim Dubois

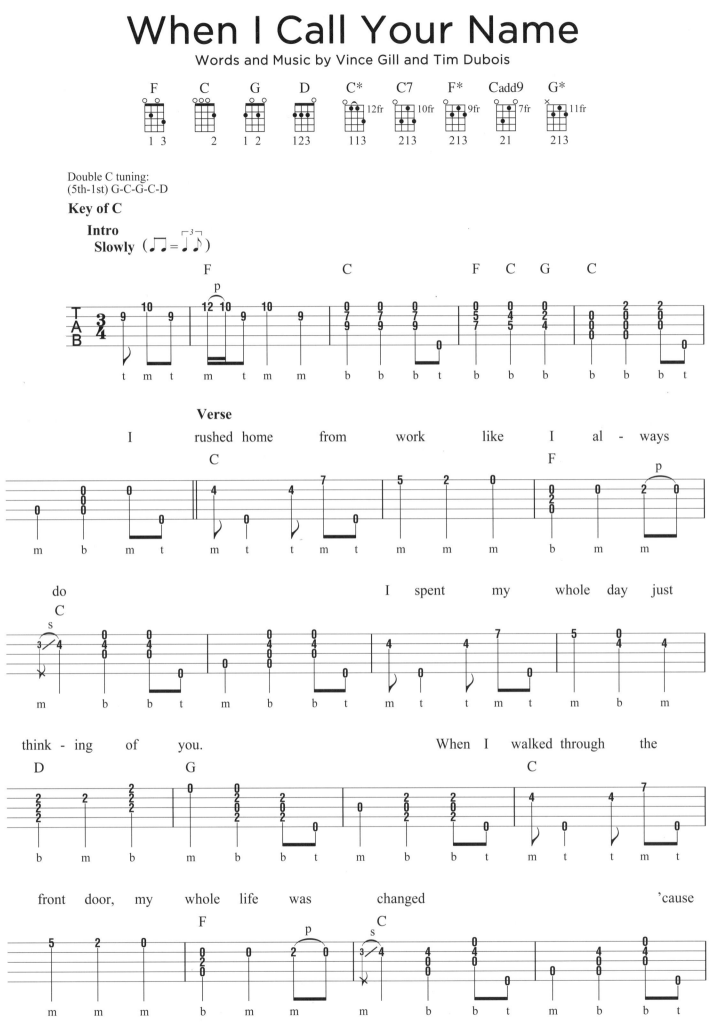

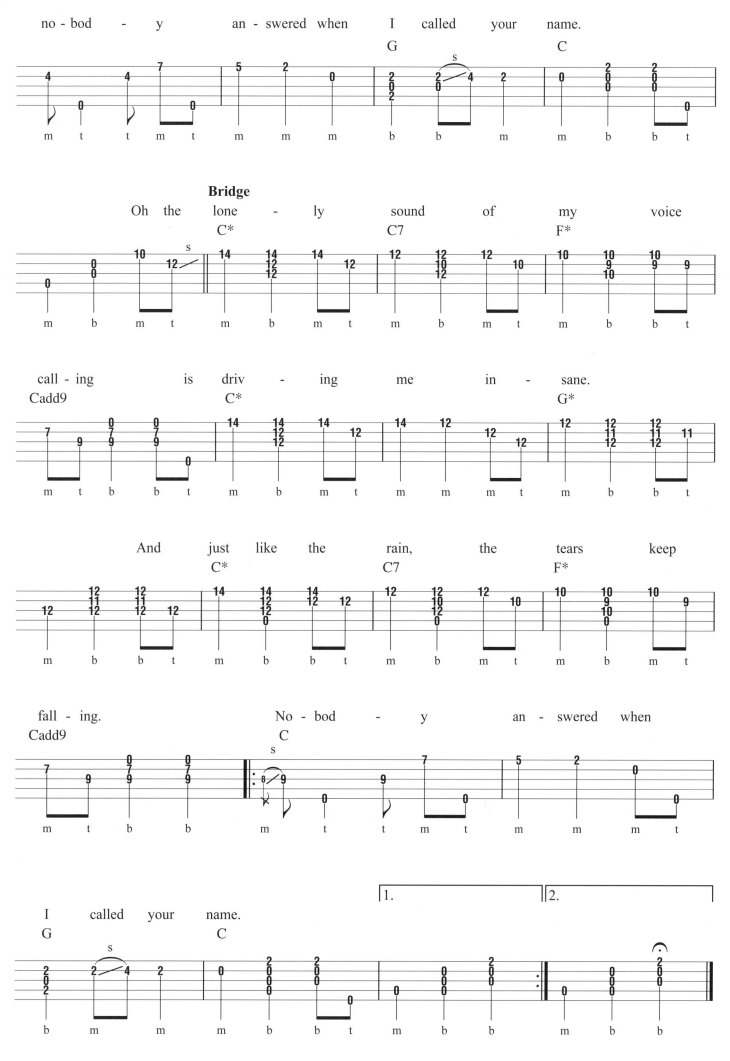

# Your Cheatin' Heart

Words and Music by Hank Williams

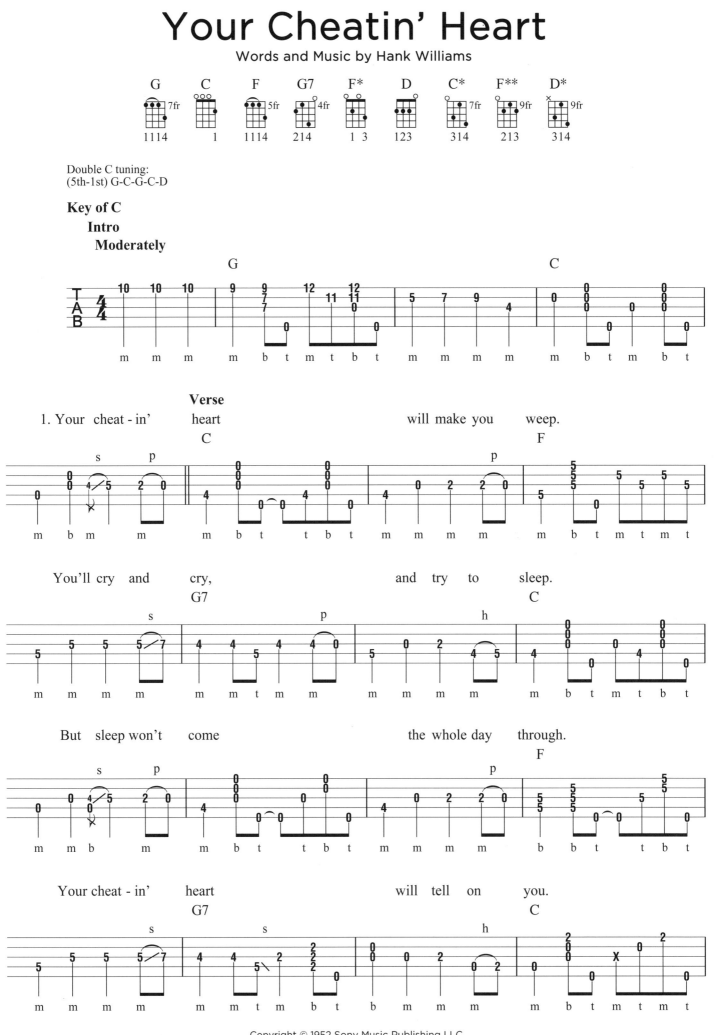

Double C tuning:
(5th-1st) G-C-G-C-D

**Key of C**

**Intro**

**Moderately**

**Verse**

1. Your cheat-in' heart will make you weep.

You'll cry and cry, and try to sleep.

But sleep won't come the whole day through.

Your cheat-in' heart will tell on you.

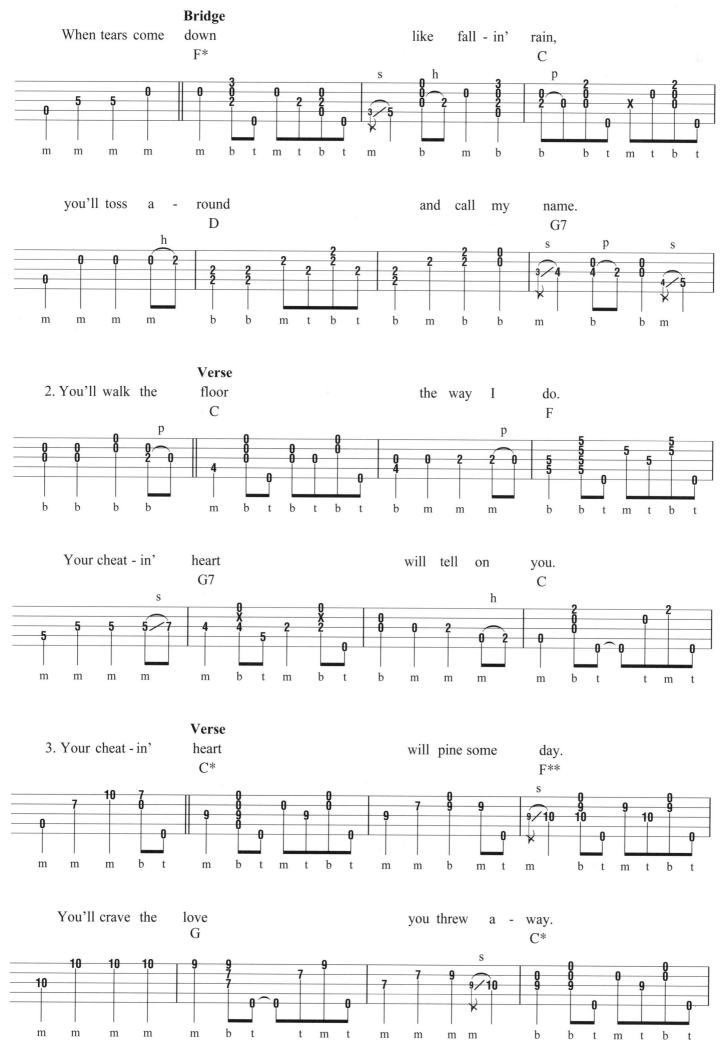

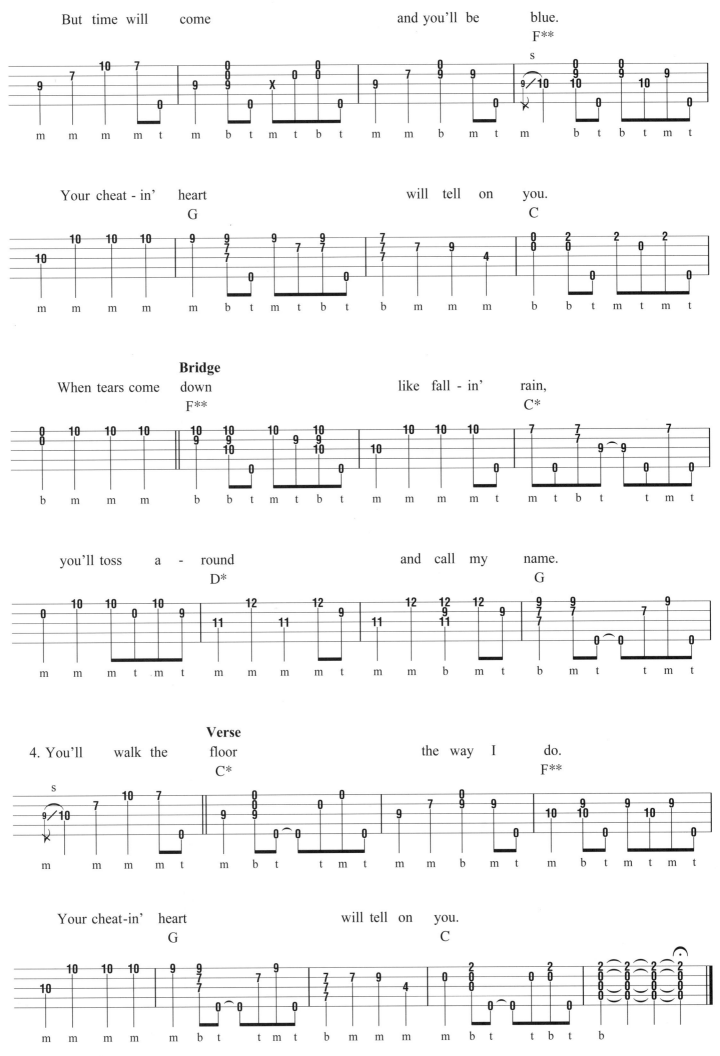